DISASTER-RESILIENT INFRASTRUCTURE

UNLOCKING OPPORTUNITIES FOR ASIA AND THE PACIFIC

APRIL 2022

ADB

DISASTER-RESILIENT INFRASTRUCTURE

UNLOCKING OPPORTUNITIES FOR ASIA AND THE PACIFIC

APRIL 2022

ADB

Contents

Tables, Figures, Boxes, and Maps

TABLES

FIGURES

BOXES

MAPS

Foreword

Disasters triggered by natural hazards threaten the long-term sustainability of development in Asia and the Pacific. Countries across the region face significant disaster and climate risk. From 2012 to 2021 alone, infrastructure failure due to insufficient resilience contributed to about 80,729 disaster-related fatalities. Extreme weather events and geophysical hazards over the same period caused direct physical losses averaging $58 billion per year, or $159 million per day. Infrastructure, homes, and businesses were damaged, with indirect economic and social consequences for jobs, productivity, and service provision.

The escalation in disaster losses underscores the urgency of addressing disaster risk adequately when planning and designing infrastructure in developing member countries (DMCs) of the Asian Development Bank (ADB). Disaster risk is an especially pressing concern, given the region's huge infrastructure investment requirements over the next 20 years, combined with the expected adverse impact of climate change, which would make extreme weather occurrences even more frequent and intense.

According to ADB's seminal report *Meeting Asia's Infrastructure Needs* (2017), developing Asia must "invest $26 trillion from 2016 to 2030, or $1.7 trillion per year . . . to maintain its growth momentum, eradicate poverty, and respond to climate change (climate-adjusted estimate)."

Clearly, therefore, infrastructure resilience presents a critical challenge for Asia and the Pacific. How and where investments are made will largely determine its ability to cope with disaster and climate risk for decades to come. Ensuring investments are risk-informed will prevent or, at the very least, reduce the impact natural hazards have on assets and systems in the region.

Since 2015, the international community's commitment to advancing disaster-resilient infrastructure has been reflected in Sustainable Development Goal 9 (build resilient infrastructure, promote sustainable industrialization, and foster innovation), global target D of the Sendai Framework for Disaster Risk Reduction (substantially reduce disaster damage to critical infrastructure and disruption of basic services), and the Principles for Quality Infrastructure Investment of the Group of Twenty (G20) countries, among others. But while upstream architecture has an important role in setting goals and providing a normative framework for resilience building, in many DMCs, greater emphasis must be placed on how they can attain the resilience objective.

This publication, intended for DMC policy makers and practitioners, accordingly explores opportunities to strengthen infrastructure resilience through practical solutions, and thus unlock significant co-benefits. Approaches to addressing the attendant challenges, beyond access to finance, are explored here. These include risk assessment, investment appraisal, operation and maintenance across the life cycle of the infrastructure asset, and overarching ways of achieving system-wide resilience objectives and implementing effective governance models.

A prosperous, inclusive, resilient, and sustainable Asia and the Pacific is a primary focus of ADB advocacy. With this publication, ADB hopes to contribute to the discourse and to encourage dialogue among its DMCs, and between the DMCs and their development partners.

NOELLE O'BRIEN

Chief, Climate Change and Disaster Risk Management Thematic Group,
and concurrently Director, Climate Change and Disaster Risk Management Division
Sustainable Development and Climate Change Department
Asian Development Bank

Acknowledgments

This publication was prepared under the Asian Development Bank (ADB) technical assistance project Building Disaster-Resilient Infrastructure through Enhanced Knowledge. Grant funding for the project came from the Japan Fund for Prosperous and Resilient Asia and the Pacific (JFPR), financed by the Government of Japan through ADB.

Steven Goldfinch, disaster risk management specialist with ADB's Sustainable Development and Climate Change Department (SDCC), provided overall guidance. Mario Unterwainig, SDCC disaster risk management specialist (resilient infrastructure), led the development of the publication with Alih Faisal Pimentel Abdul, coordinating consultant. Ghia V. Rabanal, operations analyst, and Gren J. Saldevar, senior operations assistant, both with SDCC, provided administrative support. The publication was edited by Mary Ann Asico, and layout was done by Rocilyn Locsin Laccay. Vivid Economics and the Asian Disaster Preparedness Center (ADPC) contributed to the research, gathered data, and prepared the draft report.

The publication benefited from peer reviews and detailed comments from the following ADB staff: Charlotte Benson, SDCC principal disaster risk management specialist; Nathan Rive, senior climate change specialist, Central West Asia Department; Alexandra Galperin, senior disaster risk management specialist, Pacific Department; Arghya Sinha Roy, SDCC principal climate change specialist (climate change adaptation); and Belinda Hewitt, SDCC disaster risk management specialist.

Various data sources were used. Besides the analysis and case study research from Vivid Economics and the Asian Disaster Preparedness Center (ADPC), survey data were compiled and ADB experts and stakeholders in ADB developing member countries (DMCs) across Asia and the Pacific were interviewed. These consultations have been of significant value, and ADB thanks everyone who helped in the development of this publication.

Abbreviations

ADB	Asian Development Bank
BCR	benefit–cost ratio
DAPP	dynamic adaptive policy pathways
DMC	developing member country
DRF	disaster risk financing
FRMI	Flood Risk Management Interface
GDP	gross domestic product
GFDRR	Global Facility for Disaster Reduction and Recovery
IPCC	Intergovernmental Panel on Climate Change
LTS	long-term strategy
MCA	multi-criteria assessment
MDB	multilateral development bank
MPWT	Ministry of Public Works and Transport, Cambodia
MRD	Ministry of Rural Development, Cambodia
NBS	nature-based solution
NCFA	national contingent financing arrangement
O&M	operation and maintenance
ODI	Overseas Development Institute
PPP	public–private partnership
RCP	Representative Concentration Pathway
SSP	Shared Socioeconomic Pathway
UNFCCC	United Nations Framework Convention on Climate Change

Executive Summary

Resilience is a critical challenge for developing Asia, where exposure to climate and geophysical hazards is widespread. Between 2004 and 2020, disasters caused losses of over $500 billion in the region, and affected 2.1 billion people (Sirivunnabood and Alwarritzi 2020). The risk posed by natural hazards is expected to intensify in the coming decades as economies grow, urbanize, and grapple with climate change. Resilience planning, including measures taken to reduce, transfer, and manage climate and disaster risk, will be of vital importance to developing Asia as it strives to sustain economic development and reduce poverty.

Infrastructure has a central role to play in supporting resilience. Large-scale spending on infrastructure will underpin economic development. Developing Asia will require an estimated $1.7 trillion in annual capital expenditures to meet its infrastructure needs up to 2030 (ADB 2017). The way the infrastructure investments are planned, operated, and financed will fundamentally shape resilience in the region. There are three key reasons for this. First, the infrastructure assets are likely to be exposed to hazards; choices made about their location and design will therefore determine whether and to what extent losses occur. Second, the resilience of infrastructure as a system shapes the ability of users to trade in, and gain access to, basic services in the event of a disaster: evidence from Viet Nam suggests that the knock-on economic costs from infrastructure outages can be up to twice as high as the damage to the infrastructure assets themselves (Woetzel et al. 2020). Third, infrastructure affects the geographic distribution of economic activity—and therefore the spatial profile of future development, which can take place in more or less disaster-prone locations.

This report identifies opportunities to provide resilient infrastructure across developing Asia. It draws on a survey of planners and operators, a review of the literature, and case studies on best practice, as well as two original modeling applications, to identify practical ways of improving infrastructure resilience. The work takes a holistic view of practices that affect infrastructure resilience, including risk assessment, investment appraisal, and operation and maintenance across the life cycle of an infrastructure asset, as well as overarching approaches to achieving system-wide resilience, financing, and governance objectives. Three crosscutting themes and 16 specific opportunities across these areas are identified (see Figure 2).

The first crosscutting theme of resilience enhancement is understanding and accounting more fully for its benefits. The importance of disaster risk is widely recognized in Asia and the Pacific, and routinely considered in infrastructure investment planning and prioritization. However, planning decisions are often based on a narrow and simplistic view of risk, leading to a focus on the assets, rather than on system or user resilience. The use of the Triple Dividend resilience framework for planning, involving an assessment of benefits for their potential not only to reduce disaster losses but also to boost economic development and lead to wider co-benefits, can steer decision makers toward opportunities that deliver greater value for money. In a study of water resilience interventions in developing countries, for example, 75% were found to promote economic development, and 89% to deliver societal co-benefits, such as gender inclusion (Mechler and Hochrainer-Stigler 2019). This report highlights opportunities to take a broader view of resilience benefits when defining resilience objectives and prioritizing infrastructure investments (see Opportunities 1 and 7).

The second crosscutting theme is improving risk information. While the global case for resilience is clear, local evidence of current and future risk is often insufficiently robust to support decisions. Where higher capital or operational costs are perceived to exceed the intangible, long-term, and uncertain benefits of infrastructure resilience to disasters, under-investment in resilience can result. More spatially granular information about risk—taking future demographic, economic, and climate scenarios into account, and expressed in decision-relevant socioeconomic terms—could thus improve decision-making. Approaches to overcoming existing barriers to risk information include the increased use and standardization of open-source data, and the application of dynamic adaptive policy pathways to account for future uncertainties (see Opportunities 4, 5, and 8).

Improving coordination between decision makers is the third crosscutting theme. Interconnections between infrastructure systems across different spatial, sectoral, economic and societal areas require a similarly interlinked approach to managing resilience. However, developing such an approach for the region is a formidable task: only around 50% of respondents to a survey done for this report ranked this among the top-three priority areas for enhanced practice. Early coordination between sectors, owners, and operators allows them to create a shared vision for resilience objectives and to build a common understanding of relevant hazards and their impact (see Opportunities 2 and 3). Investment decisions made at a cross-sectoral level can give more careful consideration to system-wide costs and benefits, including those that cross spatial and sectoral boundaries (see Opportunities 7 and 10). Finally, this decision-making process can be supported by integrated financial planning and institutional structures that incentivize resilience beyond the stakeholders' core sectoral or regional responsibilities, as discussed in Sections 7 and 8.

Practical solutions intended to boost resilience span all areas of infrastructure provision. The opportunities identified in this report cover risk-informed investment decisions and efficient operations, underpinned by appropriate resilience objectives and financial and institutional structures. Two original case studies on the use of open-source risk information and dynamic adaptive policy pathways (see Sections 4.5 and 5.5) show how these investment decisions are reached. Accompanying examples showcase existing best practice and demonstrate "tried-and-tested" routes to success, which can be used as blueprints to drive further progress across the region.

1 Introduction

Infrastructure development has been instrumental in strengthening economic growth in the Asia and Pacific region. Over the 5 years from 2015 to 2019, gross domestic product (GDP) grew by 6% yearly, on average (ADB 2019a).[1] More than 1.1 billion people also moved above the poverty line between 1990 and 2015 (ADB 2021b).[2] At the same time, investments in infrastructure have been significant. The People's Republic of China (PRC), a leading infrastructure investor, invests more than 15% of its GDP in infrastructure (AIIB 2020). There is strong evidence that economic growth is closely connected with infrastructure investments, and with the improvements in productivity, market access, and ability to crowd in private investment they bring about, as highlighted in Figure 1. More importantly, infrastructure is also directly associated with poverty reduction, and can lead to significant broader developmental gains alongside economic growth (ADB 2017; AIIB 2019; Willoughby 2002). As the region emerges from the global COVID-19 pandemic, infrastructure investments will therefore have a significant role in recovery and developmental progress beyond pre-pandemic levels across the region.

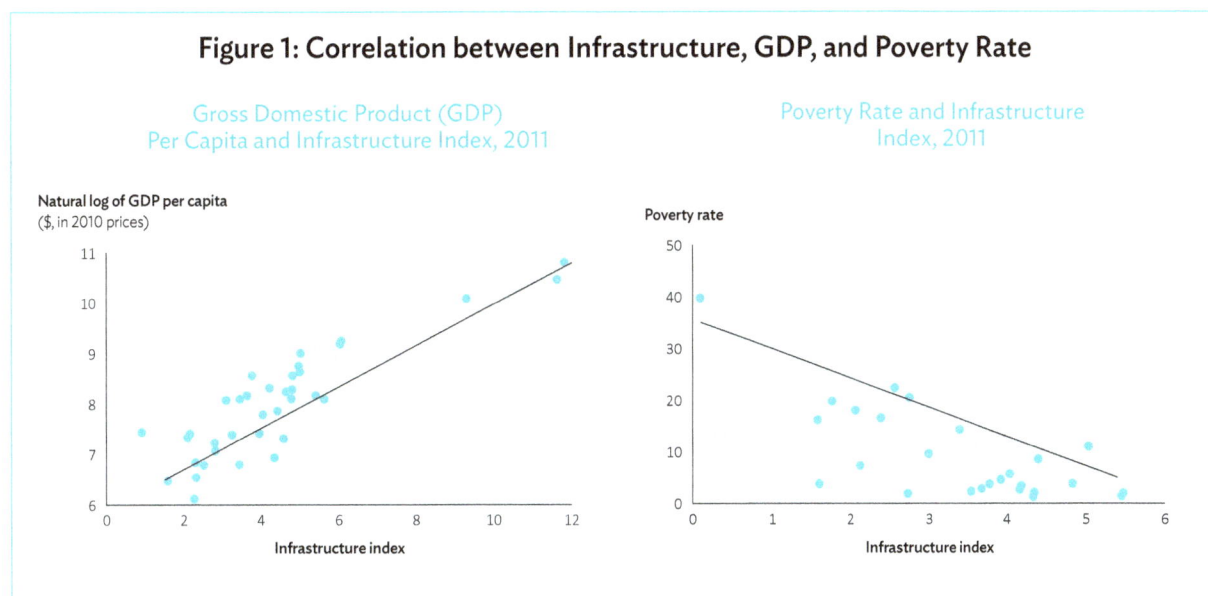

Figure 1: Correlation between Infrastructure, GDP, and Poverty Rate

Source: Based on Figures 2.1 and 2.2 in ADB (2017). https://www.adb.org/sites/default/files/publication/227496/special-report-infrastructure.pdf.
Notes: The figure shows data for developing member countries of the Asian Development Bank. The infrastructure index is computed on the basis of the first principal component of road, airport, electricity, telephone, mobile, broadband, and water and sanitation infrastructure stocks. Higher values indicate greater infrastructure availability.

However, economic growth and the infrastructure systems that underpin it are imperiled by disaster risk.
In the Asia and Pacific region, disaster risk from both geophysical and climate hazards is high. Disaster risk and its interaction with infrastructure systems vary across the region, but Map 1 shows that much of the region faces severe disaster risk from at least one hazard. Multi-hazard hot spots, to which many countries are exposed, present the largest and most complex risk (Lu 2019).

---

[1]   Data for 2020-21 is not shown due to the exceptional impact of the COVID-19 pandemic during those years, which are not reflective of long-term trends.
[2]   Measured as a reduction in the number of people living on less than $3.20 a day.

Map 1: Significant Risks to the Asia and Pacific Region from Various Hazards

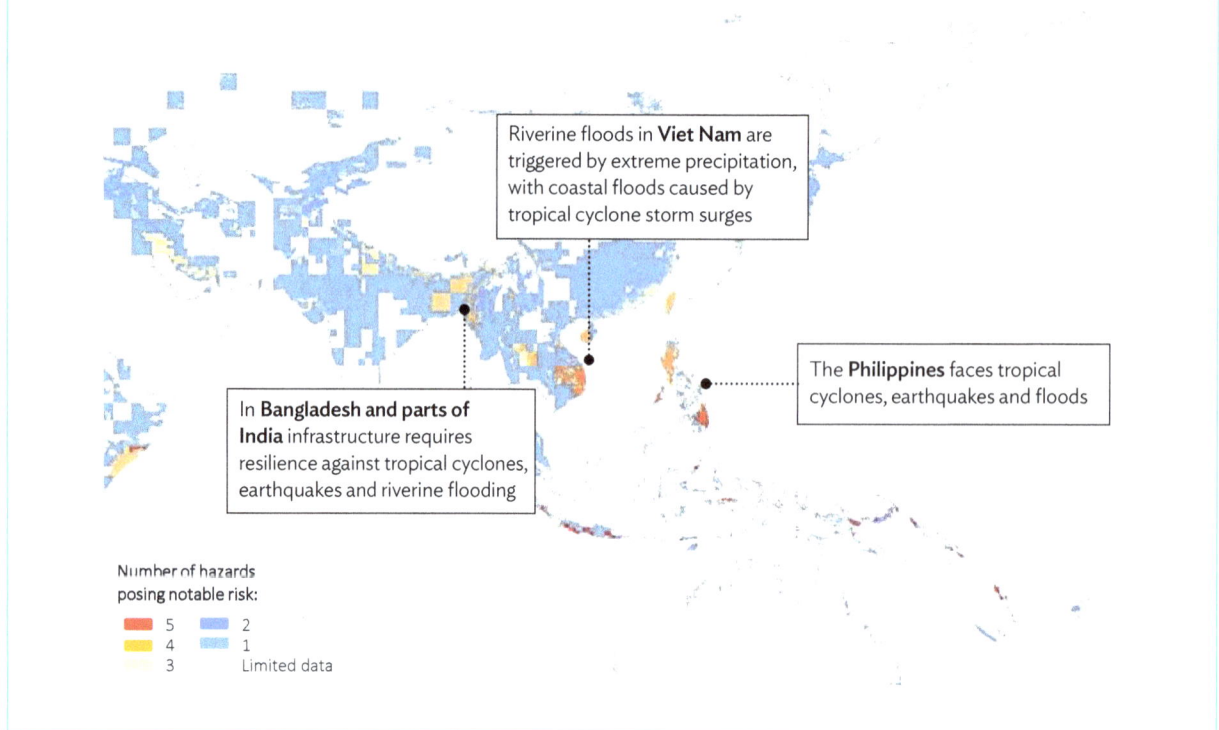

Riverine floods in **Viet Nam** are triggered by extreme precipitation, with coastal floods caused by tropical cyclone storm surges

The **Philippines** faces tropical cyclones, earthquakes and floods

In **Bangladesh and parts of India** infrastructure requires resilience against tropical cyclones, earthquakes and riverine flooding

Number of hazards posing notable risk:

- 5
- 4
- 3
- 2
- 1
- Limited data

Notes: Multi-hazard hot spots shown in the map are examples, and are not meant to be exhaustive.
Source: Vivid Economics, drawing from Dilley et al. (2005), ADB (2014), and Cheng and Chang (2009).

Disaster risks are set to increase further over the coming years and decades, as both climate and population patterns change. According to the Sixth Assessment Report of the Intergovernmental Panel on Climate Change (IPCC), heavy precipitation events are very likely to intensify and become more frequent with increased global warming (IPCC 2021). Similarly, the risk from other hazards, including tropical cyclones and coastal flooding, is expected to increase as temperatures continue to rise. In addition to this increased risk of acute disasters, climate change is projected to cause significant long-term stresses from chronic hazards, such as rising sea levels, heat waves, and drought. Sea level rise is particularly relevant to many low-lying islands in the Pacific, as well as to Asian coastal regions. Insufficiently risk-informed development, unplanned urbanization, and population growth, resulting in an increase in the number of people and the value of economic activity in hazard-exposed areas, will further heighten the risks from disasters. For example, direct infrastructure asset damage from a 1-in-100-year flood event in Ho Chi Minh City could rise from about $200–$300 million today to $500 million–$1 billion by 2050, with estimated knock-on costs to the economy rising from $100—$400 million to between $1.5 billion and $8.5 billion (Woetzel et al. 2020).

Effective investment in resilient infrastructure can support wider social and economic resilience. Reliable infrastructure services can greatly reduce the impact of disasters on economies and communities, supporting relief and recovery efforts and the provision of essential services to vulnerable groups. Investments in more resilient infrastructure in low- and middle-income countries have an average benefit–cost ratio (BCR) of 4:1, according to World Bank estimates: they deliver $4 in benefits for every $1 spent on resilience (Hallegatte,

Rentschler, and Rozenberg 2019).[3] Crucially, these investments not only lessen the impact of disasters but also foster long-term growth and poverty reduction, irrespective of disasters. Benefits to vulnerable population groups, such as women and girls, help to mitigate some of the disadvantages that generally hold back these groups. In India, for example, reliable access to electricity improves women's employment by 12% (World Bank 2019).

Infrastructure investment needs in developing member countries (DMCs) of the Asian Development Bank (ADB), estimated at $26 trillion for the 2016–2030 period, offer a unique opportunity to improve resilience across the region (ADB 2017). The unprecedented scale of the investment calls for an unparalleled focus on resilience to disasters and the long-term stresses caused by climate change. These investments, if done right, can make infrastructure systems, and the societies and economies that depend on them, much more resilient today and over the multi-decade lifetime of the infrastructure assets, even as disaster risk evolves. On the other hand, missing this opportunity to support social and economic resilience, through well-planned and well-executed infrastructure investments, can have sustained negative impact on development objectives in the region (ADB 2017).

This report identifies opportunities to improve infrastructure resilience in the region. It draws on existing literature, new insights from engagement with in-country stakeholders, and two original case studies prepared specifically for this report (see Sections 4.5 and 5.5). The opportunities are inspired by barriers that currently prevent or limit progress toward increased infrastructure resilience across developing Asia.

The report is structured around six key areas, covering all key aspects of delivering disaster-resilient infrastructure (see also Table 1):

- setting integrated, system-wide *objectives* for disaster resilience (Section 3);
- understanding and quantifying *disaster risk* (Section 4);
- prioritizing infrastructure *investments* that foster resilience (Section 5);
- ensuring the efficient *operation and maintenance* of infrastructure assets for resilience (Section 6);
- scaling up *financing* for infrastructure resilience (Section 7); and
- designing *institutions* that effectively incentivize the development of resilient infrastructure systems (Section 8)

In each of these six areas, the report provides practical guidance in addressing existing barriers faced by DMCs, by

- setting out the *role and importance* of each area in improving infrastructure resilience;
- highlighting the *current status* and key barriers that prevent progress across the region;
- offering practical guidance on *concrete opportunities* to improve the resilience of infrastructure to disasters; and
- providing examples of *successful interventions* and best practices implemented in different countries, and ways in which these could be leveraged to drive further progress.

---

[3] Median cost–benefit ratio based on analysis of infrastructure in the power, water and sanitation, transport, and telecommunications sectors in low- and middle-income countries. Ratios for individual investments may vary significantly.

Insights and opportunities developed are targeted at DMC stakeholders in three key categories: national governments, sectoral ministries, and infrastructure operators and owners. For the purposes of this report, the idealized roles of each stakeholder are assumed to be as follows (see Table 1):

- **National governments.** National administrations in DMCs, including government departments that are not directly linked to a particular infrastructure sector, such as the ministry of finance, the national planning commission, the national disaster management office, and the ministry of the environment. These stakeholders have the key role of implementing resilience-supporting policies and guiding coordination between stakeholders.

- **Sectoral ministries.** Government departments with direct links to infrastructure sectors, such as ministries of energy, water, transport, communications, and urban infrastructure. Stakeholders in these departments are responsible for providing sector-specific support and guidance to infrastructure operators.

- **Infrastructure operators and owners.** Public or private entities that provide infrastructure services—such as energy, water, transport, communication, and housing—to users. Operators and owners help ensure that resilience improvements are incorporated at all stages of the asset cycle, for example, by conducting comprehensive risk assessments, prioritizing resilient investments, and operating effectively before, during, and after disasters.

Development partners, such as multilateral development banks (MDBs) and other international organizations or donors that provide broad support for resilience efforts, also have an interest in infrastructure resilience in DMCs but are not the primary target group for this report.

Table 1: Stakeholder Roles across Key Aspects of Infrastructure Resilience

Category	National Government	Sectoral Ministries	Infrastructure Owner/Operator	Development Partners*
Asset life cycle				
Risk Assessment (Section 4)	Develop a shared understanding of critical infrastructure risks and user vulnerability. [3] Promote the use of standardized, replicable approaches to decision-relevant risk assessments. [4]		Identify and quantify disaster risks for infrastructure assets, using open-source data, risk models, and software. [5]	
Investment (Section 5)	Account for future uncertainty in planning at national scale. [8]	Contribute to effective decision-making through focus group meetings and multi-criteria assessments. [7]	Prepare a long list of all resilience, including engineering options and NBS options, and determine their cost-effectiveness. [6]	Supporting activities, including capacity building, knowledge sharing, and financial contributions
Operation and Maintenance (Section 6)	Implement credible national O&M policies, for example, minimum maintenance standards and enforcement. [9] Develop and execute well-coordinated emergency response plans.	Implement sectoral O&M policies, for example, ring-fenced budgets. [9]	Prioritize asset maintenance to avoid costly repairs, for example, through asset management systems. [9] [10]	
Enabling environment				
Objective Setting (Section 3)	Incorporate resilience objectives in long-term national development strategies and align with network-and system-wide resilience. [2]		Define priorities for resilient infrasstructure interventions, accounting for socioeonomic and environmental impact. [1]	
Finance (Section 7)	Increase availability of risk transfer finance instruments and make public funds conditional on resilient reconstruction. [13] [14] Support operators in raising funds through climate finance or private finance mechanisms for resilience, for example, by coordinating with development partners and the private sector. [11] [12]		Raise funding for resilience improvements through appropriate channels, for example, through own resources, debt, equity, transfers, or ex ante disaster risk finance mechanisms.	
Institutional Support (Section 8)	Encourage and enforce risk ownership through risk-sharing mechanisms (regulation and financial incentives). [15] Set up governance structures to guide coordination between stakeholders. [16]		Work with the public sector to agree on and implement equitable burden sharing. [15] [16]	

NBS = nature-based solution, O&M = operation and maintenance.

[x] refers to Opportunity x (see Figure 2)

* Development partners are not the primary target audience of this report. Hence, their role is not laid out in substantial detail. A separate report will be published with more in-depth guidance for multilateral development banks.

Source: Vivid Economics.

Figure 2 provides an overview of all opportunities set out in this report across the six areas, alongside the primary stakeholder group(s) at which each opportunity is targeted and the barrier faced by those stakeholders that the opportunity is expected to address.

Figure 2: Opportunities to Build Infrastructure Resilience across Asia and the Pacific

Setting objectives for disaster resilience (Section 3)

Barrier: Objectives are set with a focus on preventing asset-level loss and damage after a disaster
→ Opportunity 1: Broaden disaster resilience objectives

Barrier: Resilience investments are not consistently coordinated with development strategies
→ Opportunity 2: Integrate resilience objectives into long-term development strategies

Assessing disaster risk and potential impact (Section 4)

Barrier: Application of risk assessments to infrastructure projects is limited
→ Opportunity 3: Develop a shared understanding of critical infrastructure risks

Barrier: Quantitative analysis is insufficient
→ Opportunity 4: Promote the use of standardized, replicable approaches to making decision-relevant risk assessments

Barrier: Up-to-date, high-quality data are sparse and data access is restricted
→ Opportunity 5: Use open-source data, risk models, and software in conducting high-level risk assessments

Prioritizing infrastructure resilience investments (Section 5)

Barrier: Hard engineering solutions are often prioritized
→ Opportunity 6: Consider the use of nature-based solutions when building, upgrading, and maintaining infrastructure

Barrier: Resilience benefits are shared across stakeholders and difficult to quantify
→ Opportunity 7: Conduct stakeholder engagement and multi-criteria assessments to compare investment options

Barrier: Infrastructure has a long lifetime and climatic and socioeconomic circumstances are uncertain
→ Opportunity 8: Use dynamic adaptive policy pathways to manage future uncertainty

Operating and maintaining infrastructure to promote resilience (Section 6)

Barrier: Maintenance is de-prioritized in favor of capital spending
→ Opportunity 9: Prioritize asset maintenance to avoid costly repairs

Barrier: Critical service delivery is disrupted after disasters
→ Opportunity 10: Develop well-coordinated emergency response plans

Scaling up financing for resilient infrastructure and disaster response (Section 7)

Barrier: Climate finance is heavily focused on mitigation efforts
→ Opportunity 11: Increase use of climate finance for resilience

Barrier: Further private financing is needed to meet resilience needs
→ Opportunity 12: Mobilize private financing for resilience investments

Barrier: Risk transfer options and benefits are not clearly understood
→ Opportunity 13: Enhance the use of risk transfer instruments to improve disaster response

Barrier: Deployment of funds post-disaster can be inefficient
→ Opportunity 14: Make finance conditional on disaster recovery planning

Designing institutions to support infrastructure resilience (Section 8)

Barrier: Mismanagement of risk ownership creates moral hazard or inequitable burden sharing
→ Opportunity 15: Encourage risk ownership through risk-sharing arrangements and enforcement

Barrier: Priorities differ and decisions are decentralized
→ Opportunity 16: Set up governance structures to guide coordination between government, infrastructure operators, and financiers

Target audience — National government | Sectoral ministries | Infrastructure owners/operators

Source: Vivid Economics.

2 Scope and Approach

2.1 Scope and Sources of Analysis

The analysis underlying this report considers three types of infrastructure, across key infrastructure sectors:

- **New infrastructure** (e.g., roads, power distribution lines, water treatment plants) can be designed, built, and operated to promote resilience.
- **Existing infrastructure** may need to be retrofitted or managed differently, or built back better, to improve resilience, in the aftermath of a disaster.
- **Protective infrastructure** may need to be constructed to address the physical impact of disasters. This will involve the use of traditional engineering designs (e.g., concrete flood walls) as well as emerging alternatives, such as nature-based solutions (e.g., mangroves providing protection from flooding).

Infrastructure sectors of focus are energy (including electricity generation, transmission, and distribution), water and wastewater (collection, treatment, processing, and distribution), transport (roads, bridges, airports, ports, rail, and public transport), and communications (fixed-line, mobile, and broadband communications). For the purposes of this report, infrastructure assets and entire sectors are analyzed as part of a broader infrastructure system—a system of interconnected networks of assets, whose successful delivery of services to users is endangered if part of the overall system fails.

This report explores the resilience of infrastructure to disasters triggered by geophysical and climate hazards across the region. Geophysical hazards originate from internal earth processes, such as earthquakes or volcanic eruptions. Climate hazards are of atmospheric, hydrologic, or oceanographic origin. Examples are tropical cyclones (also known as typhoons and hurricanes) and floods, including flash floods; drought; heat waves and cold spells; and coastal storm surges. Climate hazards are subject both to natural variability and to permanent changes in climate, which can have a notable impact over the lifetime of infrastructure assets.

The risk from, and resilience to, such disasters should be considered alongside resilience to more chronic, long-term stresses faced by infrastructure systems. This is particularly important in the context of climate change, which can be expected to create or intensify such long-term stresses, for example, coastal inundation due to sea level rise. While this report is focused primarily on the impact of disaster events, long-term stresses are discussed at different points (e.g., see Section 8), and many of the barriers and opportunities identified within the analysis are relevant to the management of long-term stresses as well.

A survey of infrastructure stakeholders across the region highlighted the fact that both geophysical and climate hazards are expected to be important drivers of damage to infrastructure networks over the next 2 decades. Earthquakes were the most commonly listed primary hazard of concern among respondents, followed by riverine flooding and tropical cyclones (see Figure 3). If we add riverine flooding and flash flooding, floods would be the primary hazard of concern among respondents.

Figure 3: Natural Hazards Expected to Lead to Most Damage to Infrastructure Networks

SURVEY QUESTION:

Thinking about the next 20 years, which is the main natural hazard expected to damage infrastructure networks in your country?

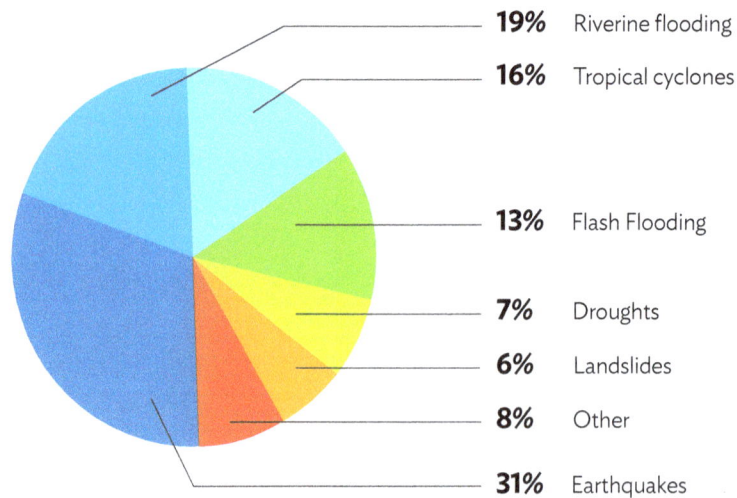

19% Riverine flooding

16% Tropical cyclones

13% Flash Flooding

7% Droughts

6% Landslides

8% Other

31% Earthquakes

Source: Vivid Economics, based on data from stakeholder survey.

A review of the existing literature and case studies was done to leverage findings from recent work in the field. The current state of play was assessed, best practices were analyzed, and barriers preventing further progress toward improved disaster resilience in DMC infrastructure across the region were identified. In particular, a World Bank report presenting a framework for understanding infrastructure resilience (Hallegatte, Rentschler, and Rozenberg 2019) and a joint policy note prepared by the World Bank's Global Facility for Disaster Reduction and Recovery (GFDRR) and the Overseas Development Institute (ODI) on the "triple dividend" of resilience (Tanner et al. 2015) provided significant insights for this analysis.

New insights were developed through a series of stakeholder engagements across the region. An extensive survey and focus group discussions with in-country stakeholders from central governments, sector departments, and infrastructure operators in DMCs across the region were used to validate and complement research findings on progress and helped to identify key barriers to further opportunities. In addition, a series of structured interviews and a validation workshop with key sectoral and regional ADB experts were held. Stakeholder engagements were conducted as follows:

- **Survey.** A 42-question survey was carried out online, to gain a better understanding of the key hazard–infrastructure interactions, progress toward resilience, and pertinent policies and key barriers in the DMCs. The survey was structured in the same way as this report to ensure that insights were gathered for each of the six key issues discussed in the following sections. During the survey period (from November 2021 to January 2022), 110 stakeholders working for infrastructure operators, sector departments, and other government ministries in Asia and the Pacific completed the questionnaire. Table 2 (Panel a) provides further details about the respondents' location and institutional affiliation.

- **Stakeholder interviews, focus group meetings, and workshop.** Interviews and meetings with stakeholders were held to discuss the state of play, challenges, and opportunities for current infrastructure resilience in the region. The discussions were guided by a questionnaire structured in accordance with the six main sections of this report, and were focused on specific country–sector contexts. The key infrastructure sectors of interest were energy, water, transport, communications, and urban infrastructure. Table 2 (Panel b) presents the themes of these discussions. A validation workshop with ADB experts was also held to provide further insights into practical challenges and emerging solutions in the DMCs.

Table 2: Summary Statistics of Stakeholder Engagements

Panel a: Number of survey respondents by location and institutional affiliation

Region*	Infrastructure Operator	Infrastructure Sector Department	Other Government Ministry	Total
Central and West Asia	0	1	10	11
East Asia	2	4	2	8
South Asia	2	10	22	34
Southeast Asia	2	15	35	52
Pacific	0	0	5	5
Total	6	30	74	110

Panel b: Sector-country pairs that were used to structure focus group meetings

Developing Member Country	Energy	Water	Transport	Communications	Urban	Cross-sectoral
Bangladesh	✔	✔	✔	✔	✔	
Nepal	✔	✔	✔	✔		
Fiji						✔
Indonesia						✔

* Note: Regions as defined by ADB. Stakeholders across 39 developing member countries (DMCs) were consulted; responses were received from stakeholders in 21 DMCs.
Source: Vivid Economics.

Survey respondents identified improvements in risk information (Section 4) and investment prioritization (Section 5) as key areas to improve infrastructure resilience. More than 80% of respondents listed at least one of these two areas as a key area (see Figure 4).

Figure 4: Survey Results on Areas for Improvement to Increase Infrastructure Resilience

SURVEY QUESTION:

What is the primary area in which improvements are required to achieve infrastructure resilience in your country?

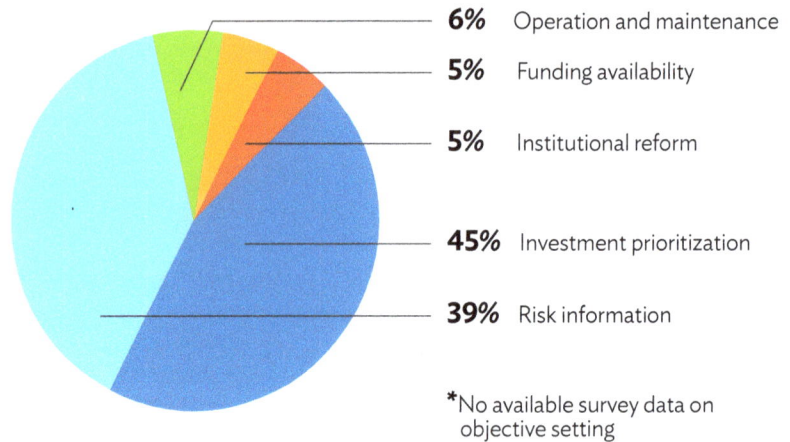

6% Operation and maintenance

5% Funding availability

5% Institutional reform

45% Investment prioritization

39% Risk information

*No available survey data on objective setting

Source: Vivid Economics, based on data from stakeholder survey.

To complement the survey findings, two original modeling exercises for the most important areas for resilience improvement identified by in-country stakeholders were conducted specifically for this report. The modeling exercises provided practical examples of how advanced techniques can be made an integral part of resilience planning. Specifically, they set out a replicable approach to

- leveraging open-source data and risk models for assessing risk and identifying critical assets, based on a road network exposed to earthquake risk in Pakistan (Section 4.5); and

- developing adaptive plans to take into account future uncertainties in prioritizing investments, based on different road-raising options for managing flood risk in Cambodia (Section 5.5).

2.2 Dimensions of Infrastructure Resilience and Benefits

Infrastructure resilience is the ability of infrastructure systems to resist, absorb, accommodate, and recover from hazards to which they are exposed—and to mitigate the impact of such events on the users served by the systems (UNDRR, n.d.[a]). It includes the resilience of users under both current and changed (by development, climate change, or other factors) conditions. As discussed in the preceding section, this report is specifically focused on infrastructure resilience to disaster events; however, the concepts described in this section also apply more broadly to other aspects of resilience.

Resilience is a property of infrastructure systems that includes not only the performance of individual assets but also their collective role in providing essential services to users. Infrastructure services are interconnected, and disruptions to the usability of specific assets can affect production, trade, or the delivery of essential services, leading in turn to broader economic or social impact. A system-wide approach takes these interdependencies into account, and prioritizes interventions with regard to their effect on risks to people and the economy, rather than to individual assets (see Figure 5). This report is focused on how infrastructure systems can reduce these risks to people and the economy, and hence ultimately support the resilience of users.

Figure 5: A System-wide Approach to Infrastructure Resilience

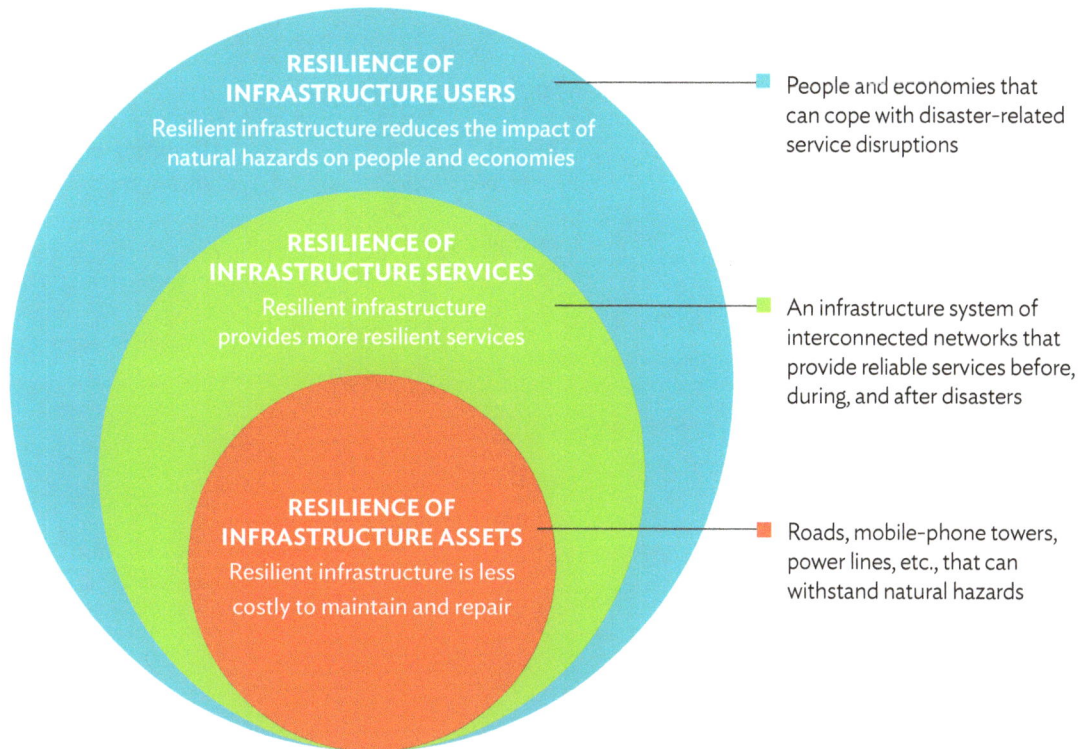

RESILIENCE OF INFRASTRUCTURE USERS
Resilient infrastructure reduces the impact of natural hazards on people and economies

■ People and economies that can cope with disaster-related service disruptions

RESILIENCE OF INFRASTRUCTURE SERVICES
Resilient infrastructure provides more resilient services

■ An infrastructure system of interconnected networks that provide reliable services before, during, and after disasters

RESILIENCE OF INFRASTRUCTURE ASSETS
Resilient infrastructure is less costly to maintain and repair

■ Roads, mobile-phone towers, power lines, etc., that can withstand natural hazards

Source: Hallegatte, Rentschler, and Rozenberg (2019), adapted by Vivid Economics.

System-wide infrastructure resilience can deliver a "triple dividend" (Hallegatte, Rentschler, and Rozenberg 2019), reducing disaster losses while also enhancing social and economic development. The Triple Dividend framework describes the benefits of infrastructure resilience in three categories (see Figure 6):

- avoiding damage and losses,
- unlocking economic potential, and
- generating development co-benefits.

Benefits in the aftermath of a disaster are realized through the first dividend—the avoidance of damage and loss. These post-disaster benefits are most commonly considered when assessing resilience benefits and prioritizing interventions accordingly. However, resilience also delivers benefits before a disaster, and irrespective of its occurrence. Reduced risks can unlock economic development by incentivizing investment by households and firms, fostering entrepreneurship, and motivating long-term planning by reducing the risk of disruptive disaster impact across longer time horizons. In many instances, interventions made to improve resilience also generate co-benefits, for example, improvements in gender equality or enhancements in natural capital. This report looks into how infrastructure provision can deliver benefits across all three categories of resilience.

Figure 6: Triple Dividend of Infrastructure Resilience Investments

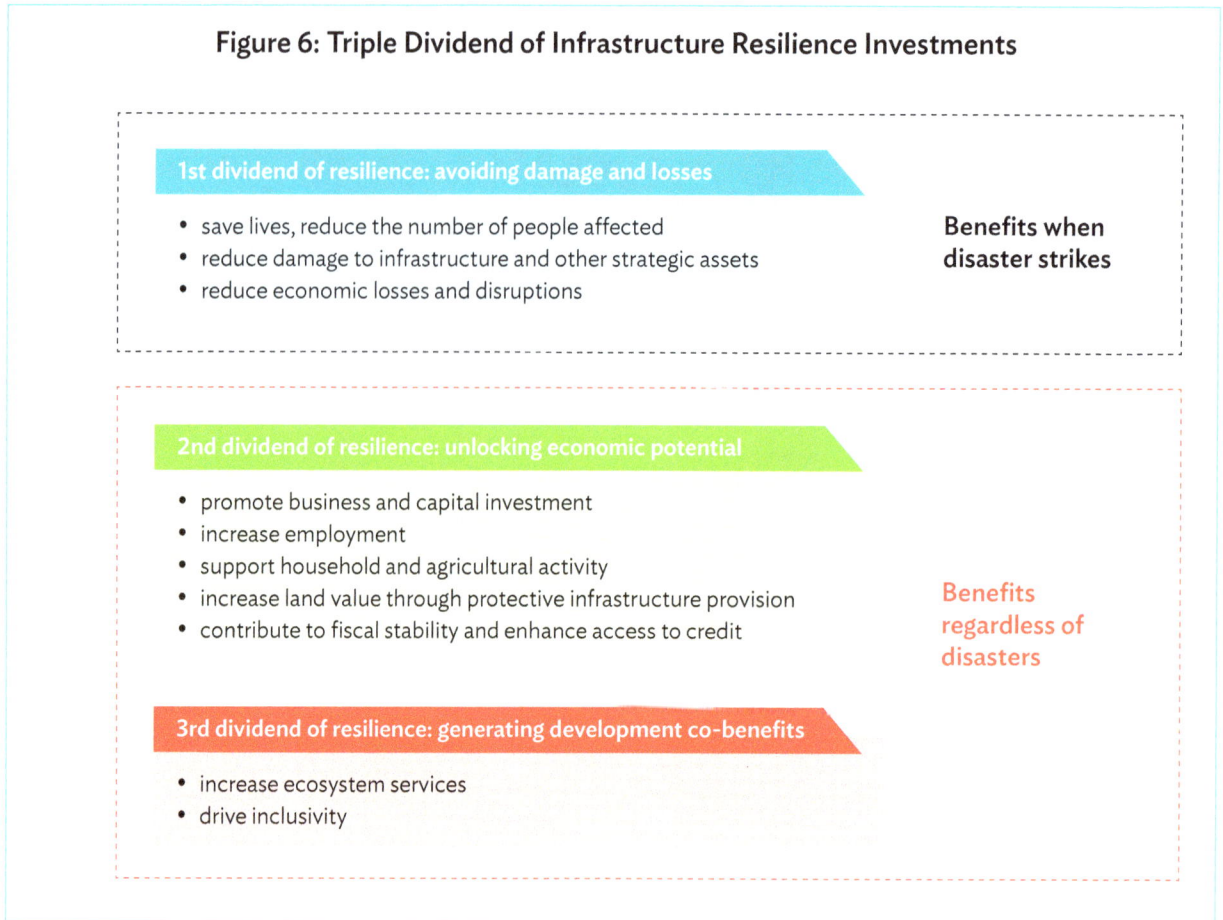

1st dividend of resilience: avoiding damage and losses

- save lives, reduce the number of people affected
- reduce damage to infrastructure and other strategic assets
- reduce economic losses and disruptions

Benefits when disaster strikes

2nd dividend of resilience: unlocking economic potential

- promote business and capital investment
- increase employment
- support household and agricultural activity
- increase land value through protective infrastructure provision
- contribute to fiscal stability and enhance access to credit

Benefits regardless of disasters

3rd dividend of resilience: generating development co-benefits

- increase ecosystem services
- drive inclusivity

Source: Tanner et al. (2015), adapted by Vivid Economics.

While the benefits of the second and third dividends of resilience are hard to quantify, and resilience interventions are often explicitly targeted only at benefits from the first dividend, survey results suggested that the interventions deliver significant benefits across all three categories (Mechler and Hochrainer-Stigler 2019). For example, a study of the benefits from 40 interventions with the primary aim of reducing disaster risk in developing countries found that 89% of water management interventions resulted in additional development co-benefits (third dividend), and over 75% unlocked economic potential (second dividend).

3 Setting Disaster Resilience Objectives

3.1 Overview

Objectives define priorities for infrastructure investment, operation, and asset management. This section discusses how objectives can be set in order to promote resilient outcomes for users and unlock the "triple dividend" of resilience.

Clear objectives are needed to ensure that infrastructure resilience is prioritized consistently and effectively. Clearly defined objectives allow project managers and policy makers to evaluate accurately the progress made and to support the continuous improvement of the infrastructure resilience strategy.

Resilience objectives can be set with a holistic view of the "triple dividend" of direct and downstream benefits of infrastructure resilience in mind. As described in Section 2, infrastructure resilience can deliver broad and systemic benefits, beyond reduction in damage and loss to individual infrastructure assets. For effective decision-making, all prospective benefits must be considered in the objective-setting process.

A shift toward a more system-wide approach to objective setting can unlock more opportunities for DMCs than an objective-setting approach that is concerned purely with asset-level resilience. An integrated system approach to promoting and protecting resilience reflects the role of the asset within the broader infrastructure system, or the connections between this system and other sectors of the economy, and goes beyond asset-level damage and losses (ADB 2021c). Interviews with stakeholders indicated the importance of such a holistic, coordinated approach for infrastructure resilience. Setting holistic, coordinated objectives is a key first step in this approach. It lays the foundation for ensuring that investments in support of systemic resilience are effectively prioritized in subsequent investment planning and appraisal processes.

Figure 7 summarizes the key opportunities and related barriers identified in this section.

Figure 7: Setting Objectives for Disaster Resilience—Barriers and Opportunities

Setting holistic, coordinated objectives	
Barrier: Objectives are set with a focus on preventing asset-level loss and damage after a disaster	**Barrier:** Resilience investments are not consistently coordinated with development objectives
Opportunity: Broaden disaster resilience objectives	**Opportunity:** Integrate resilience objectives into long-term development strategies

Source: Vivid Economics.

3.2   Opportunity 1: Broaden Disaster Resilience Objectives

Setting objectives that encompass a broad range of social, economic, and environmental benefits promotes decision-making that prioritizes these outcomes more effectively. By taking all types of resilience-building benefits into account, such an approach strengthens the business case for resilience and unlocks greater funding. It also drives more effective investment decisions and can foster buy-in from a broader range of stakeholders, making resilience a priority across sectors and allowing coordinated sector responses.

Stakeholders can systematically map out their objectives according to the Triple Dividend framework. This framework's structured approach ensures that all resilience benefits across all three dividends are actively considered in setting resilience objectives, and hence also in making subsequent decisions. Figure 8 presents Viet Nam's eight resilience objectives for the management of the Mekong Delta (see Box 1), mapped out according to the Triple Dividend framework—a practice that could be replicated.

Sharing this holistic map of resilience objectives across sectors can ensure that system-wide implications are taken into account. Improved and institutionalized channels of communication across sectors can have an important role in defining a holistic vision of resilience for infrastructure users. Formalized platforms and networks bringing together experts from different sectors to discuss and set objectives for system-wide resilience can offer a useful structure for consistent coordination on key matters (see also Section 8).

Box 1: Viet Nam's Prime Ministerial Resolution Seeks to Reduce Disaster Risk alongside Developmental and Environmental Objectives

In 2017, Viet Nam's Prime Minister issued a resolution for the "sustainable and climate-resilient development" of the Mekong Delta, and defined a set of objectives for 2050. The eight objectives span several aspects of resilience and can be framed according to the Triple Dividend framework. In fact, increased per capita income, a high level of economic progress and social organization, and the development and preservation of natural ecosystems are among the objectives, in addition to the reduction of risks from natural hazards, as shown in Figure 8. Overall, these objectives are aimed at reducing disaster risk, encouraging economic development, and protecting the environment—the "triple dividend."

While disaster risk reduction is a key objective, resilience co-benefits and economic potential are also recognized as key target areas.

Sources: Smajgl (2018); Government of Viet Nam (2017).

Figure 8: Resilience Objectives for the Management of the Mekong Delta

1st dividend of resilience: avoiding damage and losses

- Disaster risks are reduced for the people and the economy.

Benefits when disaster strikes

2nd dividend of resilience: unlocking economic potential

- Per capita income is higher than the national average and people's livelihood is secured.
- A highly developed region of the country has an advanced level of social organization.

3rd dividend of resilience: generating development co-benefits

- Ecological agriculture is developed, with the high technology agriculture rate reaching over 80%.
- Forest cover increases to 9% of national territory (compared to the current 4.3%).
- Important natural ecosystems are preserved and developed.
- Synchronous development of socioeconomic infrastructure, modern urban systems, and road and waterway transportation systems allows the country to avoid system conflicts with irrigation and dike systems.
- Irrigation infrastructure develops in harmony with the transformational model of agricultural production, adapting to climate change, especially in ecological subregions.

Benefits regardless of disasters

Note: Ecological agriculture designates agricultural practices that improve the strengths of natural ecosystems as agro-ecosystems, for food and fiber production. It includes promoting biodiversity and ensuring the sustainability of production (Magdoff 2007).
Sources: Vivid Economics; Mekong Region Futures Institute.

3.3   Opportunity 2: Integrate Resilience Objectives into Long-Term Development Strategies

To maximize co-benefits and advance broader development objectives more sustainably, infrastructure resilience can be made a central feature of national development strategies. The provision of infrastructure influences patterns of spatial or sectoral development, and thus plays a central role in shaping development outcomes. Since development objectives typically depend on resilience (for example, in avoiding losses that lead to entrenched poverty, or in securing reliable access to key export markets), infrastructure resilience objectives may be specifically aligned with outcomes promoted in national development strategies. Integrating infrastructure resilience objectives into development strategies in this way can help to ensure that the benefits are recognized and aligned with development strategies and that they are prioritized by key decision makers.

The alignment of resilience objectives with broader long-term adaptation needs and their integration with those needs will also be more certain. The Updated Philippine Development Plan 2017–2022 (NEDA, Philippines, 2017) (Box 2) explains in detail the role of infrastructure resilience.

Infrastructure resilience could be further mainstreamed into national strategies, thus allowing synergies of resilience and development to be exploited to their full extent. The role of infrastructure is not systematically addressed as a central component in national strategies. A review of long-term strategies (LTSs) showed that infrastructure resilience is currently not a central theme in most instances. It is therefore less likely to be an explicit target of investment plans based on those strategies. Disaster risk management offices, development ministries, and financing offices tend to work in silos, and resilience objectives for specific infrastructure sectors are defined separately from development strategies, according to stakeholder interviews done for this report. Without close integration across these functions, opportunities to advance development objectives through investments in infrastructure resilience are likely to be underestimated or missed entirely.

Long-term development strategies offer a practical way of explicitly recognizing the role of infrastructure resilience and aligning it with wider developmental objectives. Infrastructure resilience and disaster risk management are key components of adaptation. LTSs articulate countries' efforts to meet the reductions in greenhouse-gas emissions laid down in the Paris Agreement. Including resilience objectives in documents like the LTSs can help in setting clear targets and mapping out the steps needed to achieve them. Furthermore, given the stand-alone role of infrastructure resilience in development, integrating resilience objectives into development strategies shows commitment from the highest levels of government and recognition of this role. Integration can signal demand and thus stimulate private sector financing. Clear identification of resilience needs can also help leverage national and international adaptation finance channels for infrastructure (see Opportunity 11) (Tall et al. 2021). Making disaster risk management a prime concern of government can help to establish this link and give higher priority to infrastructure resilience. International agendas like the Sendai Framework for Disaster Risk Reduction 2015–2030 (UNDRR 2015) can reinforce these priorities and provide additional practical guidance.

Integrating infrastructure resilience objectives into development strategies also enables a better understanding of complementarities, as well as overlaps and potential misalignments, across infrastructure and development plans. This understanding can improve alignment between infrastructure and development plans, and in turn unlock increased buy-in and funding from different stakeholders.

Box 2: Philippine National Development Plan Targets Infrastructure Resilience in Key Sectors

In the Updated Philippine Development Plan 2017–2022, reducing vulnerability to climate change and to natural hazards is a strategic objective. Infrastructure resilience, together with the necessary investments, receives priority, in light of its recognized importance in poverty reduction and economic development.

The plan also recommends the development of infrastructure that supports both resilience and development objectives. This includes irrigation systems to improve the productivity and climate resilience of agriculture, and regional seaports to promote trade and provide redundancy in the transport network as a disaster response strategy.

This example shows how national development plans can spell out the potential of infrastructure resilience to support development objectives and make use of this potential in infrastructure planning.

Source: NEDA, Philippines (2017).

4 Assessing Disaster Risk and Potential Impact

4.1 Overview

To promote infrastructure resilience, decision makers need to understand how disaster risk affects and is affected by infrastructure systems. This section looks into how risk assessments can improve awareness and understanding of disaster risk.

Disaster risk reflects the likelihood and severity of hazards and their effect on vulnerable assets, people, and production. Key components of disaster risk are shown in Figure 9. The definitions of risk components in this section conform to those provided in the Glossary at the end of this report (before the References section).

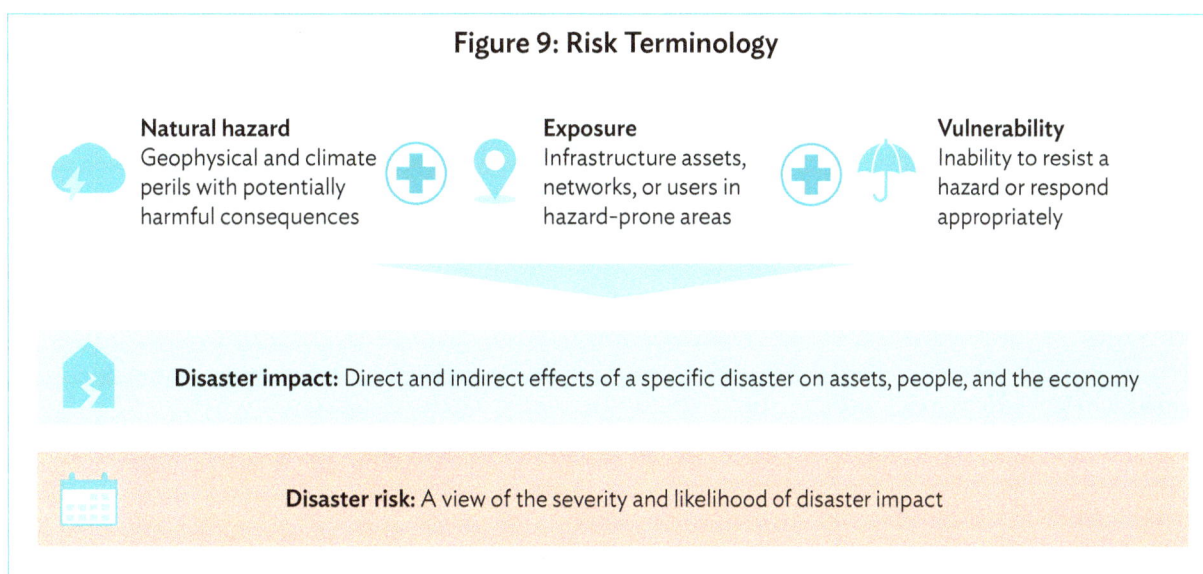

Figure 9: Risk Terminology

Natural hazard
Geophysical and climate perils with potentially harmful consequences

Exposure
Infrastructure assets, networks, or users in hazard-prone areas

Vulnerability
Inability to resist a hazard or respond appropriately

Disaster impact: Direct and indirect effects of a specific disaster on assets, people, and the economy

Disaster risk: A view of the severity and likelihood of disaster impact

Source: Vivid Economics.

Risk assessments involve analyzing how hazards give rise to impact, to support decision-making. A robust understanding of disaster risk is the foundation of an effective assessment of the resilience benefits associated with interventions in infrastructure systems. If risks are not understood properly, subsequent prioritization decisions may lead to suboptimal resilience outcomes and miss important opportunities to reduce or manage risks cost-effectively. The communication sector of Bangladesh, where fire hazards are not considered adequately despite the country's high level of exposure, as reported by stakeholders during a focus group meeting, is an example. The most effective risk assessments therefore consist of the following:

- **Identifying risks** and how these shape impact. A qualitative analysis is made of causal chains between hazards and impact, taking into account the factors that intensify or mitigate these links, for example, exposure, vulnerability, and the possibility of compounding disasters. Risk identification allows decision makers to formulate options for managing risks and improving system-wide resilience.

- **Quantifying risks**, in terms of the likelihood and severity of hazard impact. Risks may be quantified in terms of their expected impact, or their impact in events of any frequency (for example, the expected impact of a 1-in-10-year event).

Risk identification pins down current and future sources of risk, and how these affect and are affected by infrastructure systems. This process can begin with an account of relevant hazards, the frequency of events of varying severity, and the extent to which infrastructure assets are exposed and vulnerable. Risk identification also includes an assessment of the potential for compound disasters, for example, an earthquake followed by a landslide. How impact on infrastructure propagates to the rest of the economy and to the wider society can then be considered, to form a view of how impact of interest is shaped by hazards. Lastly, the risk identification process can look into how risk factors are expected to change over time, as a result of climate change, urban growth, technological progress, or other circumstances. These high-level insights into the relevance and impact of risk can be combined into a summary of the key channels of impact to be managed.

Risk quantification informs long-term decision-making by allowing resilience investment costs to be viewed in the context of potential losses from inaction. Once the most relevant risks have been identified, quantification helps in assessing in more detail the likelihood of disasters and the magnitude of their impact on infrastructure, people, and the economy. Expressing these factors in numerical and monetary terms, through cost–benefit analyses and other systematic approaches to evaluating options, supports efficient decision-making. How hazards give rise to impact and how the impact varies across space and time must typically be modeled for this purpose.

The outcomes of the risk assessment are communicated to stakeholders, using metrics relevant to the recipients' needs. The metrics should depend on the reach and nature of decisions made by each stakeholder. For example, the potential financial costs associated with disaster damage may be most relevant to infrastructure operators and financiers, who make asset resilience decisions, while national governments may be more interested in the wider impact of improved resilience on people and the economy.

Survey respondents considered risk assessment a key area where improved practice could enhance resilience. Sixty-eight percent of respondents identified better risk assessments among the three most important improvements needed to enhance infrastructure resilience in their country overall; 39% said it was the most important factor. These survey results imply that progress made in improving risk assessments could have a significant impact not only on raising awareness but also on actively strengthening resilience.

Three areas of improvement to overcome key barriers to scaling up the availability and quality of risk assessments were identified:

- **Access to up-to-date, high-quality data.** Survey respondents regarded better access to up-to-date, high-quality data as the most needed enhancement in risk assessments. For example, according to focus interviews, many risk assessments in the energy sector of Bangladesh are based on 30- to 40-year-old data, or on assumptions that fail to capture the changing circumstances over the lifetime of assets. The use of open-source data and models (see Opportunity 5) can support entities in conducting risk assessments that are both realistic and rigorous.

- **The case for risk assessments.** This was the second-most-named improvement needed for better risk assessments. In the focus group discussions, it was noted that whether or not risk assessments are conducted, and to what extent, depends on the scale and focus of the infrastructure investment: large national projects are more likely to be subject to a comprehensive risk assessment than smaller, rural projects. The process should become more replicable and less costly once standardized methods have been developed (see Opportunity 4), thereby allowing risk assessments to be made for all infrastructure projects in the future.

- **Quantitative assessment of risks and impact.** Survey results showed that risk assessments currently give qualitative consideration to a broad range of relevant aspects (including potential areas of impact and infrastructure damage), but less than half involve quantitative assessment (see Figure 10). Focus interviews also revealed technical challenges in understanding the complex interactions between risk and the infrastructure system, and in modeling future risk. For instance, in private sector risk assessments made in Nepal's water sector, classifying infrastructure risk merely as "low"/"medium"/"high" fails to capture the complexity of the risk. Developing a shared understanding of critical infrastructure risks (see Opportunity 3) will be a stepping-stone to modeling relevant factors more comprehensively and in a quantitative fashion.

Figure 10: Current State of Risk Assessment Practices in Asia and the Pacific

SURVEY QUESTION: Which of the following components are analyzed as part of the risk assessment procedure in your country and sector?

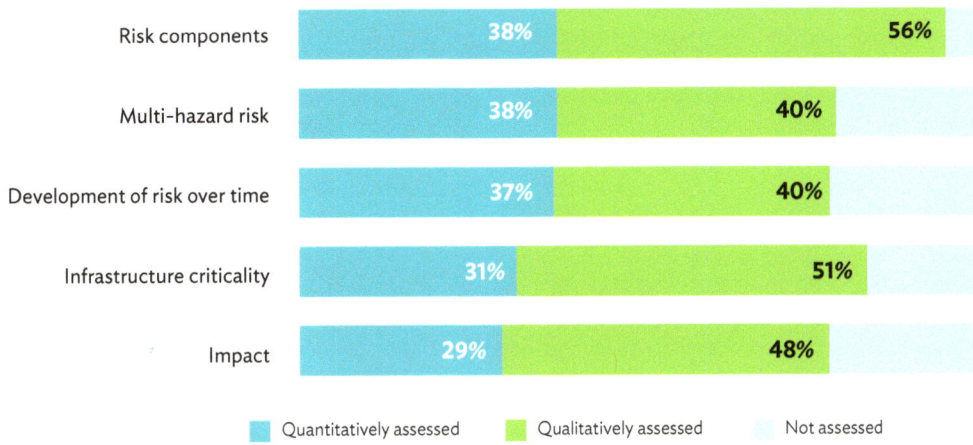

Component	Quantitatively assessed	Qualitatively assessed
Risk components	38%	56%
Multi-hazard risk	38%	40%
Development of risk over time	37%	40%
Infrastructure criticality	31%	51%
Impact	29%	48%

Quantitatively assessed　　Qualitatively assessed　　Not assessed

Source: Vivid Economics, based on data from stakeholder survey.

Figure 11 provides an overview of the practical steps in conducting a comprehensive risk assessment, based on key takeaways from stakeholder engagements and literature, and maps these onto key opportunities for progress presented in later sections. Risk identification is explored in more detail in Section 4.2 (Opportunity 3), and risk modeling to inform quantification, in Section 4.3 (Opportunity 4).

Figure 11: Practical Guide to Risk Assessment

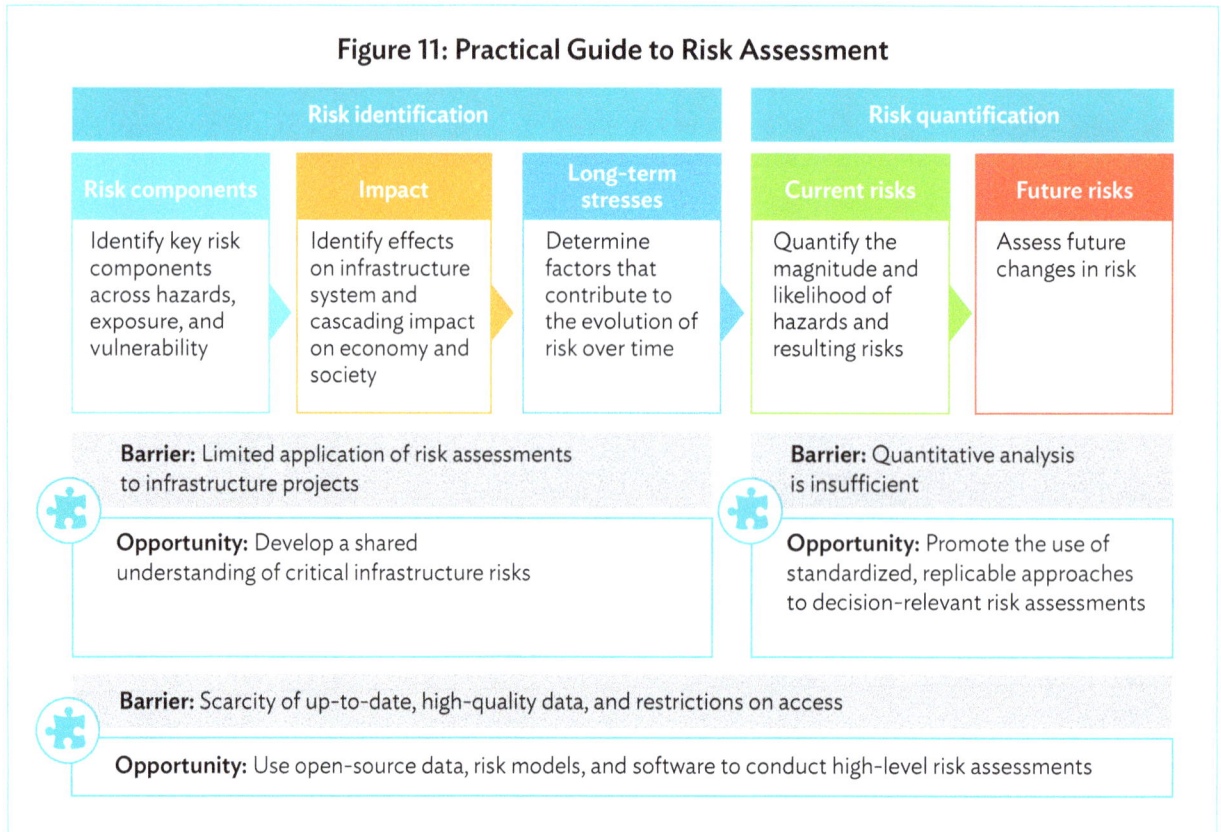

Risk identification			Risk quantification	
Risk components	**Impact**	**Long-term stresses**	**Current risks**	**Future risks**
Identify key risk components across hazards, exposure, and vulnerability	Identify effects on infrastructure system and cascading impact on economy and society	Determine factors that contribute to the evolution of risk over time	Quantify the magnitude and likelihood of hazards and resulting risks	Assess future changes in risk

Barrier: Limited application of risk assessments to infrastructure projects

Opportunity: Develop a shared understanding of critical infrastructure risks

Barrier: Quantitative analysis is insufficient

Opportunity: Promote the use of standardized, replicable approaches to decision-relevant risk assessments

Barrier: Scarcity of up-to-date, high-quality data, and restrictions on access

Opportunity: Use open-source data, risk models, and software to conduct high-level risk assessments

Source: Vivid Economics.

4.2 Opportunity 3: Develop a Shared Understanding of Critical Infrastructure Risks

Identifying risks is an important first assessment step in understanding risks and prioritizing their subsequent modeling. The key components of disaster risk, their impact on the infrastructure system and beyond, and stresses that could affect the risk components over time are determined. Risk identification can provide governments, infrastructure owners, and operators with a shared qualitative understanding of key issues and their importance, even before more quantitative insights become available through subsequent risk modeling. This initial assessment phase (i) helps operators and users to understand how risks propagate throughout systems and shape outcomes, and (ii) guides subsequent modeling and quantification efforts.

However, risk identification is often not given the importance it deserves, such that suboptimal outcomes are obtained. Risk identification is often not pursued by, or shared systematically with, infrastructure operators. Survey results suggested that the greatest challenge in developing a comprehensive understanding of disaster risk is insufficient capacity to conduct risk assessments due to more pressing demands on time and budgetary resources (cited as the biggest challenge by almost half of the respondents). In Nepal's transport sector, for example, risk assessments are part of environmental impact assessments, but they generally cover only some types of roads and hazards (often only landslides and flooding). As a result, stakeholders may underestimate the severity of disaster risk and may find it difficult to identify effective solutions at the asset, system, and user level.

National risk assessments provide an overview of disaster risk and thus serve as a guide for infrastructure planners in developing a more in-depth, location-specific risk analysis. National-level assessments identify the key drivers of disaster risk, such as the main hazards, exposure, and vulnerabilities in the national infrastructure sectors. Subnational authorities and infrastructure operators can use these findings as a starting point for developing more detailed risk assessments for specific infrastructure projects, as risks may vary substantially, depending on the location and type of infrastructure. In Indonesia, earthquake maps prepared by the Ministry of Public Works from stakeholder interviews are the main standard for seismic risks and enable a joint understanding of disaster risk.

The first step in identifying risks is understanding the various risk components at the asset level: types of hazards, infrastructure exposure to those hazards, and infrastructure vulnerability. Risk assessments are typically based on these three components, whose interaction determines the overall level of risk faced by an infrastructure asset (see Table 3).

- **Hazards.** Risk assessments identify the types of hazards (singular and compound) that can occur in the region or country of interest, as well as their likelihood and severity profile. This process includes scoping the potential evolution of existing hazards and the emergence of new hazards over time.

- **Exposure.** To assess the exposure of infrastructure assets, policy-makers need to know where the infrastructure assets are located relative to areas at risk from specific hazards.

- **Vulnerability.** The vulnerability of an asset is typically a function of its nature, age, quality, upgrades, and reinforcements, and the existence of protective infrastructure.

The next step in risk identification is aimed at understanding the wider socioeconomic impact on user resilience. The reliance of other systems and a variety of user groups on infrastructure services allows hazard impact to cascade and multiply. Insufficiently resilient infrastructure networks can expose users to disaster risk. Planners must consider the scale to which users are affected by the failure of infrastructure operators to provide the expected services. The following considerations provide a starting point for looking into these types of indirect impact:

- **What are the potential implications of users' inability or reduced ability to gain access to infrastructure services?** The implications range from unfavorable health outcomes (for example, those due to diminished access to clean, piped water) to a decline in economic activity (due, for example, to road damage, and hence workplace inaccessibility).

- **What are the demographic characteristics of the people who are likely to be affected by infrastructure failure?** These include both the total number of users and the factors that render them more or less vulnerable to a reduction in infrastructure services, such as income, age, and gender. For example, reduced access to sanitation may have more severe impact on children, who are at higher risk of diarrheal diseases.

According to the focus group discussions, the Fiji government has been able to develop a good understanding of disaster impact on people by making use of information shared via social media. Opportunities to leverage similar information-sharing channels may increase as technology progresses.

Lastly, long-term stresses must be considered to make risk identification relevant to forward-looking decision-making. Infrastructure investment decisions have long-term implications because assets are long-lived and asset risks and vulnerabilities can have irreversible impact on spatial and sectoral patterns of economic development. Risks evolve dynamically and are subject to various layers of uncertainty. Factors contributing to the evolution of risk over asset lifetimes need to be identified in order to consider how risk profiles will affect long-term development and economic objectives. Long-term stresses are factors that change hazards, exposure, vulnerability and impact over time. Understanding how risk trajectories may jeopardize long-term development objectives can help governments in identifying suitable resilience solutions and planning for contingencies. Key long-term stress factors to consider include the following:

- **long-term stresses affecting hazards** (climate change, loss of biodiversity, pollution);

- **long-term stresses affecting exposure** (demographic pressures in high-risk areas, number and location of infrastructure assets, interconnectedness of infrastructure network, technological change); and

- **long-term stresses affecting vulnerability and impact** (insufficient building standards or investment in resilience measures, more intensive asset use than designed, fueled, for example, by population growth, urbanization, and economic growth).

Table 3: Key Components of Disaster Risk Assessment

Item	Risk components			
	HAZARD	**EXPOSURE**	**VULNERABILITY**	**IMPACT**
Examples of risk components in Asia and the Pacific	Tropical cyclones	Coastal location	Asset built to insufficient standards to withstand hazard	Reduced user access to infrastructure services
Long-term stresses affecting risk components	Climate change	Increasing asset base	Population growth and urbanization, leading to more intensive asset use than designed	

Source: Vivid Economics.

Box 3: Strategic Identification of Risk Drivers—The Philippine Development Plan 2017–2022

The Philippines' national development plan for 2017–2022 highlights the importance of incorporating risk assessments into infrastructure planning at all levels of government, to protect assets. The plan recommends a range of measures for identifying drivers of risk. These include disseminating national hazard maps and geospatial information about climate change and disaster exposure, developing risk estimation models and loss and damage databases, and mapping ecosystems that contribute to resilience.

Under the Strategic Framework for Reducing Vulnerability of Individuals and Families, the Philippines will conduct a nationwide vulnerability and risk assessment. This assessment will be organized and led by the Philippine Climate Change Commission, which will also assist local communities in carrying out the assessment. The findings will enable local communities to identify their risks and vulnerabilities and to develop local climate and disaster risk strategies, while also creating a broader picture of the risk facing the country overall.

Additionally, according to the national development plan, a resilience index will be developed for each area on the basis of its

- exposure to hazards,
- ability to mitigate the impact of risks, and
- ability to recover from the risks if they materialize.

This index will have the same baseline value as the 2018 resiliency index, so that the government can gauge overall progress.

The national development plan emphasizes the importance of ensuring infrastructure resilience, through disaster risk reduction and climate adaptation strategies, when considering infrastructure investments. The assessments of local vulnerability and risk will allow the government to incorporate risk and vulnerability analysis seamlessly into infrastructure plans. For example, as stated in the national development plan, a national master plan for flood and drainage, to be developed and implemented by the government, will include region-specific projects based on an area's vulnerability to floods.

Source: NEDA, Philippines (2017).

4.3 Opportunity 4: Promote the Use of Standardized, Replicable Approaches to Making Decision-Relevant Risk Assessments

Risk assessment outputs must be transparent and actionable in order for stakeholders to benefit from the analysis. The main purpose of the risk assessments is to inform decisions regarding infrastructure investment, operation, and maintenance. The assessments must therefore deliver clear, relevant, and actionable outputs on which the decisions of governments and infrastructure operators can be based.

In practice, however, risk assessment results may not be systematically targeted at specific decision-relevant criteria; investment prioritization could, as a result, be suboptimal. Model outputs in the form of hazard maps, exposure scores, or future scenarios are difficult to interpret and may not be directly linked with investment prioritization criteria. Decision-relevant factors—such as financial and humanitarian indicators, as well as probability distributions over impact of differing severity—may be missed in existing assessment frameworks. For instance, only two-thirds of respondents reported that decisions about infrastructure resilience measures were based on risk assessments. If assessment outputs exist in a vacuum instead of being integrated into decision-making, opportunities to leverage risk information in investment and operation/maintenance decisions may not be realized. As a result, investment prioritization may favor measures that are less suited to addressing the risks in question.

Standardized approaches to risk quantification are replicable and offer easy-to-use solutions for implementing cost-effective risk assessments with actionable outputs. New approaches to high-level risk assessments reduce complexity and effectively inform strategic decisions, such as spatial, sectoral, and temporal prioritization of interventions (see Box 4 below for an example). These methods are designed to be replicable and easy to use, while retaining the rigor required for reliable quantification of disaster risk. The types of resulting outputs can be targeted at the needs of decision makers to ensure that they are informative and actionable. Also, once carried out, these approaches can be applied in a new context, sector, or geography—another inherent advantage that effectively reduces the resource requirement for every additional risk assessment. Kathmandu, Nepal, where a dedicated team conducts surveys, develops the risk assessment design, and estimates costs, is an example showing standardized approaches working in practice.

The first step in risk modeling is quantifying the components of current risks. The following standardized methods could be applied (see, for example, the Pakistan case study in Section 4.5):

- **Hazard modeling.** Recent occurrences can be mapped for this purpose. For example, a heat map of days without rainfall (to model drought) or of days with extreme temperatures (to model heat waves and cold spells) could be drawn up. Similarly, acute hazards (for example, floods, earthquakes, or cyclones) could be mapped to show their location, frequency, and magnitude. Hazard mapping will indicate where "hot spots" occur.

- **Asset exposure modeling.** To model asset exposure, the hazard map described above must be overlaid with the infrastructure network map (for example, one showing the network of roads or water distribution). Assets in locations identified as hot spots are more exposed to the relevant hazard.

- **Asset vulnerability modeling.** Asset vulnerability depends on the nature of the sector and the hazard as well as on the condition of the infrastructure. In this step, sector-level vulnerability is first identified; for example, communication infrastructure may be highly vulnerable to storms but less so to droughts. Then, if the condition, age, and level of protection of each asset are known, these data can be used to inform the metric further. Combining the data with earlier maps of asset exposure results in asset vulnerability scores. Assets that are exposed and in poor condition have the highest scores.

Next, the direct and indirect impact of current risks is modeled. A practical guide to this quantification follows:

- **Direct impact on assets.** The direct impact on assets is measured in terms of the physical damage caused by hazards (in monetary value) and can be modeled with the use of past damage data or approximated in terms of asset vulnerability.

- **Indirect impact on the economy and society.** This step is crucial in determining user vulnerability. Typically, an asset criticality analysis can be done to measure indirect impact—the importance of the asset in delivering value to users. In this analysis, the first step is determining the extent to which the functioning of the whole infrastructure network depends on each individual asset. Then, the infrastructure network map must be overlaid with the key economic and humanitarian metrics of interest, for example, population density or GDP. The last step is assessing how many people or how much GDP would be at risk if a particular asset were to shut down, thus establishing dependencies within the infrastructure network.

Following the quantification of current risks, future risks are modeled through the prediction of long-term stresses, as laid out in Opportunity 3. This step involves the following:

- **Collecting predictions of future risks under various scenarios.** Some metrics that evolve over time are hazards (due to climate change), asset exposure and vulnerability (due to infrastructure investment), and indirect impact on the economy and society (due to population growth and economic development).

- **Assessing the extent to which risks and impact evolve over time under various scenarios.** This involves running through the above steps once more for each scenario being considered. The results will give an indication of the possible evolution of the likelihood and severity of impact in the future.

Lastly, results, typically centering on direct and indirect impact, must be formulated clearly to be incorporated into decision-making processes. In order for risk assessments to be decision-relevant, they must not only have the right technical input but also be embedded in broader implementation strategies for the sensitive management of the implications of assessment results. Often, this calls for highlighting all no-regret investment options or ordering infrastructure assets according to the need for disaster-proofing to withstand potentially harmful impact. Decision-relevant metrics, such as direct and indirect impact from inaction, help governments and operators to identify the resilience measures that should be prioritized. While there is some overlap, metrics of interest depend on the relevant stakeholders. Some focus metrics for each stakeholder are summarized below:

- **National government.** Impact of inaction on people and the economy, including reduced economic activity, deaths, injuries, and other health impact, as well as the distribution of this impact across demographic groups and income strata.

- **Sectoral ministries.** Impact of inaction on the network and its users, including strains on key infrastructure assets within the network created by the need to compensate for other localized failures, and effects of service failures on users.

- **Infrastructure owner/operator.** Impact of inaction on assets, including expected damage and financial implications of restoring services in a timely fashion.

- **Financiers.** Impact of inaction on operators' liquidity and the profile (amount, timing of disbursement, etc.) of required financing for disaster response.

- **Wider society.** Impact of inaction on different aspects of people's lives, including housing, health, and employment. This communication has been difficult, according to stakeholder interviews, in Fiji, where communities had to be relocated because of projected sea level rise, inundation, and tidal movement. Some households, not fully understanding the scale of the risk, were reluctant to act.

Box 4: Multi-hazard Risk Assessment—Flood Risk Modeling for the Viet Nam Road Network, 2019

This World Bank project analyzed the risks posed by floods and landslides to the Vietnamese road network, and the evolution of risk under various climate change scenarios. It identified critical roads and their vulnerability, using a network model, and combined the findings with hazard exposure data to calculate potential annual damage. The project also applied economic modeling to estimate the economic losses from road damage.

This high-level risk assessment laid out a strategy and vision for climate-resilient transport in Viet Nam, and a prioritization evaluation framework for future transport resiliency investments. With these outputs, the risk modeling can become a viable input in infrastructure investment decision-making in the country.

Source: Oh et al. (2019).

4.4 Opportunity 5: Use Open-Source Data, Risk Models, and Software in Conducting High-Level Risk Assessments

While data availability has been improving, limited access to risk-relevant data remains a challenge for comprehensive risk assessment. As described under Opportunity 4, risk data are the foundation of any risk assessment. Improvements in data availability open up the possibility of eventually being able to leverage big data for risk assessments, but access to relevant information is still limited. Lack of (user-friendly) data may compel a reduction in the scope of risk models or the use of other metrics to approximate missing variables.

Open-source data and models often prove to be of sufficient depth to deliver high-level quantitative insights regarding user vulnerability and impact. Detailed risk modeling cannot always be carried out because of technical or resource constraints. Open-source data and tools enable risk modeling with limited capacity, avoiding license fees and making free updates generally accessible as knowledge of evolving risks grows over the lifetime of infrastructure assets. The information obtained from publicly available models and data can be validated by stakeholders to help policy-makers decide whether a more extensive risk assessment or resilience strategy is needed for a high-level, quantitative understanding of risk. The multi-hazard risk assessment of critical infrastructure for Asian countries that was done at a high level to inform the practical applications in this report (Sections 4.5 and 5.5) yielded results supporting the conclusion that roads were the main type of infrastructure at risk. Moreover, the risk models and assessments, based on open-source data, can be updated easily and regularly as new information reflecting the growing knowledge of evolving risks over the lifetime of infrastructure assets becomes available.

While high-level quantification can be a catalyst for subsequent, more detailed analysis, however, it does not take the place of localized risk assessments. Using open-source data for high-level risk modeling provides a helpful overview of the risk hot spots and priority hazards in a larger region, but more in-depth analyses that take into account unique local conditions not captured in generic models are needed. For example, stakeholder interviews for this report brought out difficulties in modeling risks in Nepal's energy sector despite the availability of high-accuracy models, due to the Himalayan region's unique topology, sediments, and disaster exposure.

Besides using open-source platforms, governments and institutions are increasingly becoming involved in providing risk data to facilitate risk assessments. A variety of online platforms provide risk data free of charge (see Box 5 for an example). But public bodies do also get increasingly involved in distributing data. For example, by making national hazard maps available, the Philippine government makes it easier for other organizations to conduct risk modeling, as they do not have to model hazards themselves. Similarly, the Intergovernmental Panel on Climate Change (IPCC) provides projections of climate change scenarios (IPCC, n.d.); these were used in measuring future hydrometeorological hazards with the help of the Viet Nam risk model. Other hazard data providers with global coverage are the World Bank's Climate Change Knowledge Portal (World Bank, n.d.[b]) and the Copernicus Climate Data Store (Oasis, n.d.). More time and resources can be saved as hazard data become more available.

Box 5: Oasis Open-Source Risk Modeling

The Oasis Loss Modelling Framework (2021) is an open-source catastrophe modeling platform that provides environmental risk data and tools needed for developing and running catastrophe models at scale. This platform includes an interface for running catastrophe models as well as a toolkit for developing and deploying the model.

Recently, the Oasis Loss Modelling Framework was used in modeling flood catastrophes in the Philippines and cyclones in Bangladesh. The project's output will form the basis for a risk assessment that will be used by the insurance industry.

Sources: BMU, Germany (2018); Oasis (n.d.).

A practical application showing how (and which) open-source data can be used in conducting a high-level risk assessment for Pakistan's road network is described in the next subsection.

4.5 Application: Asset Criticality Assessment of the Seismic Resilience of Roads in Pakistan

The socioeconomic impact of the loss of service from an asset is determined by the importance of that asset to users. In other words, it relates to the extent to which users depend on the asset for trade or access to essential services. This subsection brings out a way of understanding the concept of asset criticality and applying it to an assessment of earthquake risk to roads in Pakistan, using publicly available data sources. It is based on original analysis conducted by Vivid Economics for the purposes of this report.

The approach follows five steps:

- **Step 1:** Identify hazards, exposure, and vulnerability.

  - **The scope depends on the impact of interest to the decision maker.** From a government's perspective, for instance, the scope of interest would likely include benefits of the infrastructure asset that go beyond its financial returns, such as the extent to which it supports the local economy, or the connectivity of vulnerable populations.

  - **The assessment performed here adopts the perspective of a policy-maker at the national government level.** Understanding the hazard thus requires mapping out the footprint of earthquakes of different magnitudes across the country. The exposure corresponds to the length of road that may be damaged by earthquakes of varying levels of severity countrywide. User vulnerability pertains to the people who depend on the essential services provided by each road, which could be disrupted when the asset in question is exposed to earthquakes.

- **Step 2:** Understand impact on infrastructure systems and cascading impact pathways affecting the economy and society (see also Map 2 and Map 3).

  - **Hazards do not have the same impact on all assets.** For instance, a mud road may be washed out by a 1-in-10-year flood event, whereas a hospital building would suffer only minimal damage. In the example considered, the relevant hazard footprint is the intersection of earthquake risk with soil liquefaction risk, as the co-occurrence of these events is most likely to damage roads.[4] The earthquake and soil liquefaction data come from publicly available datasets published and maintained by Columbia University's Earth Institute and the United States Geological Survey (USGS).

  - **The hazard footprint is overlaid with the road network to allow road segments exposed to earthquake risk to be identified.** The roads mapped out comprise motorways; primary, secondary, and tertiary roads; trunk roads; and links between these. Their location and characteristics were obtained from OpenStreetMap.

---

[4] Earthquake risk is defined as a greater-than-10% chance of more-than-2 m/s^2 acceleration per 50-year period, or a history of magnitude-5-or-above earthquake events with an epicenter within a 100-km radius. Soil liquefaction is a phenomenon that reduces the strength and stiffness of saturated soil in response to stress, such as shaking during an earthquake. This process causes the solid material to behave like a liquid. (Source: University of Washington, USA, n.d.)

Map 2: Mapping Hazards and Roads in Pakistan

Mapping earthquake footprint

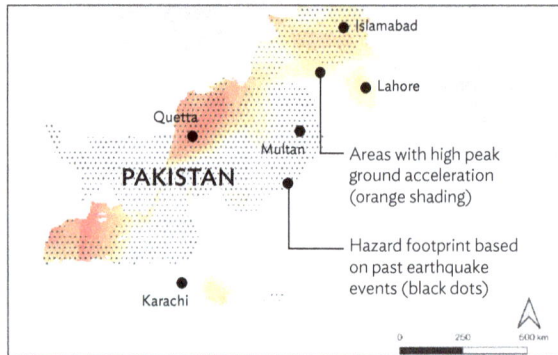

Mapping soil liquefaction risk

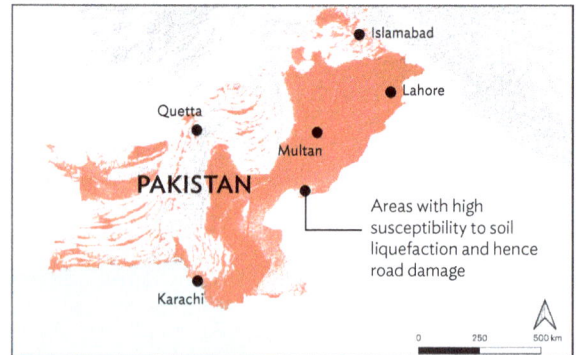

Areas with high peak ground acceleration (orange shading)

Hazard footprint based on past earthquake events (black dots)

Areas with high susceptibility to soil liquefaction and hence road damage

Mapping roads

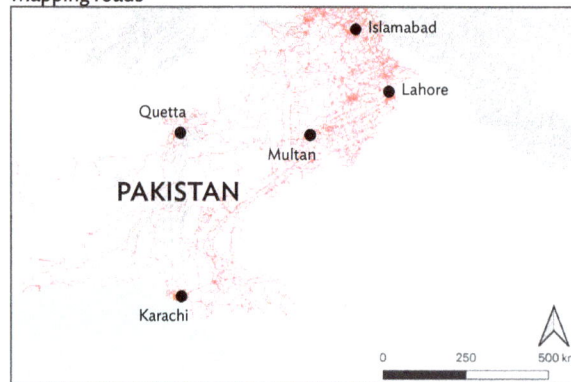

Note: Zone delimiters in the maps on the top indicate the extent of hazard footprints within the area analyzed and are not intended to represent geopolitical boundaries. The bottom map highlights road segments used in the analysis which are not intended to represent geopolitical boundaries

Source: Vivid Economics.

- To identify impact pathways related to socioeconomic outcomes, the services rendered by the infrastructure asset to the local community and economic activity must first be clearly understood. Roads, like other transport infrastructure assets, provide access to markets and essential goods and services. The services rendered by each segment of road within a country depend on the location of other assets. For instance, a road can provide access to other essential services, such as hospitals. If there are other roads in the vicinity, then the given segment serves a smaller area.

- Overall, four dimensions of access are considered and modeled with the help of publicly available datasets. First, the area of influence, or catchment area, of each road segment is modeled; a network model of junctions and road segments is used for this purpose. Four dimensions of road services are then quantified: economic, as the GDP of the catchment area; social, as the share of vulnerable populations in the area; connectivity, as the number of hospitals and schools that would be cut off in the event of a disaster; and remoteness, as the population that depends solely on the road for access to the wider region, represented by the size of the segment's catchment area (Aalto University, Finland, n.d.; HDX, n.d.[a], n.d.[b], and n.d.[c]; WorldPop 2020.

Map 3: Catchment Areas of Road Segments in Pakistan

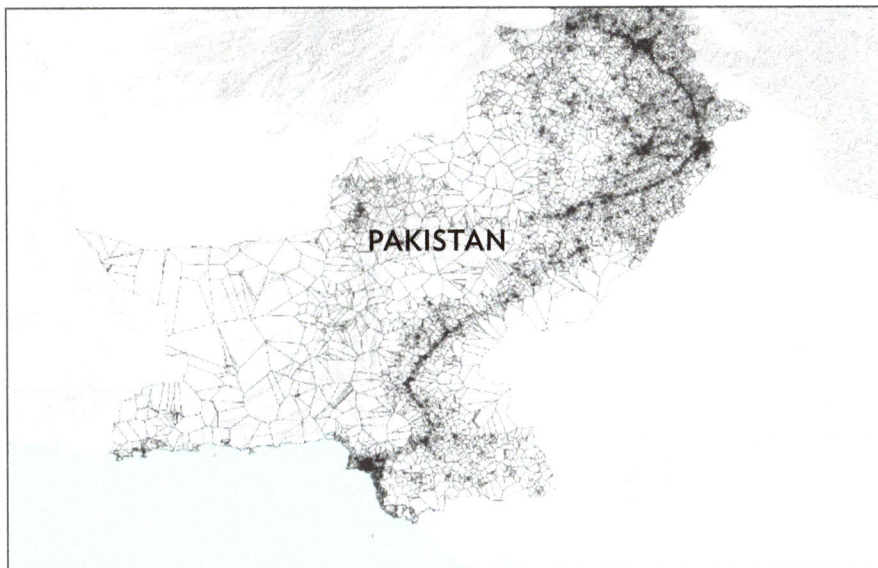

Source: Vivid Economics.

- **Step 3:** Identify long-term stresses.
  - **Future changes in risk may be driven by climatic or socioeconomic uncertainty.** Earthquakes are not a climatic hazard; uncertainty around climate change pathways is therefore not relevant to the analysis presented here. Uncertainty over socioeconomic outcomes, on the other hand, could affect the assessment. For instance, if the Baluchistan region were to experience higher growth than Punjab over the next 50 years, it could become a more highly relevant region for investment than it is at present.

- **Step 4:** Quantify the magnitude and likelihood of current risks (see Map 4).
  - **Quantifying the magnitude of the risk requires bringing together the different quantified measures of hazard, exposure, and vulnerability.** Mapping out the road segments in areas exposed to both earthquake and soil liquefaction risk can bring together the hazard and exposure metrics. An index that gathers together the four dimensions of services rendered by roads must be created to aggregate the vulnerability metrics. A threshold of the vulnerability index can be used in defining the roads that are considered as critical. The intersection of the critical and exposed roads, in turn, provides a unique metric for understanding the magnitude of risk in the country. For instance, in Pakistan, critical and vulnerable roads are found mostly in the Punjab region.
  - **Different hazard footprints can be represented for different severity levels, to understand the likelihood of risk.** This was not done here to avoid overcomplicating the analysis. The severity level for hazards can be expressed in different ways, through return periods (which indicate the likelihood that an event of a given severity will occur in a given year), hazard-specific metrics (such as the Richter scale for earthquakes), or other representations.

Map 4: Identifying Critical Road Segments Exposed to Earthquake Risk in Pakistan

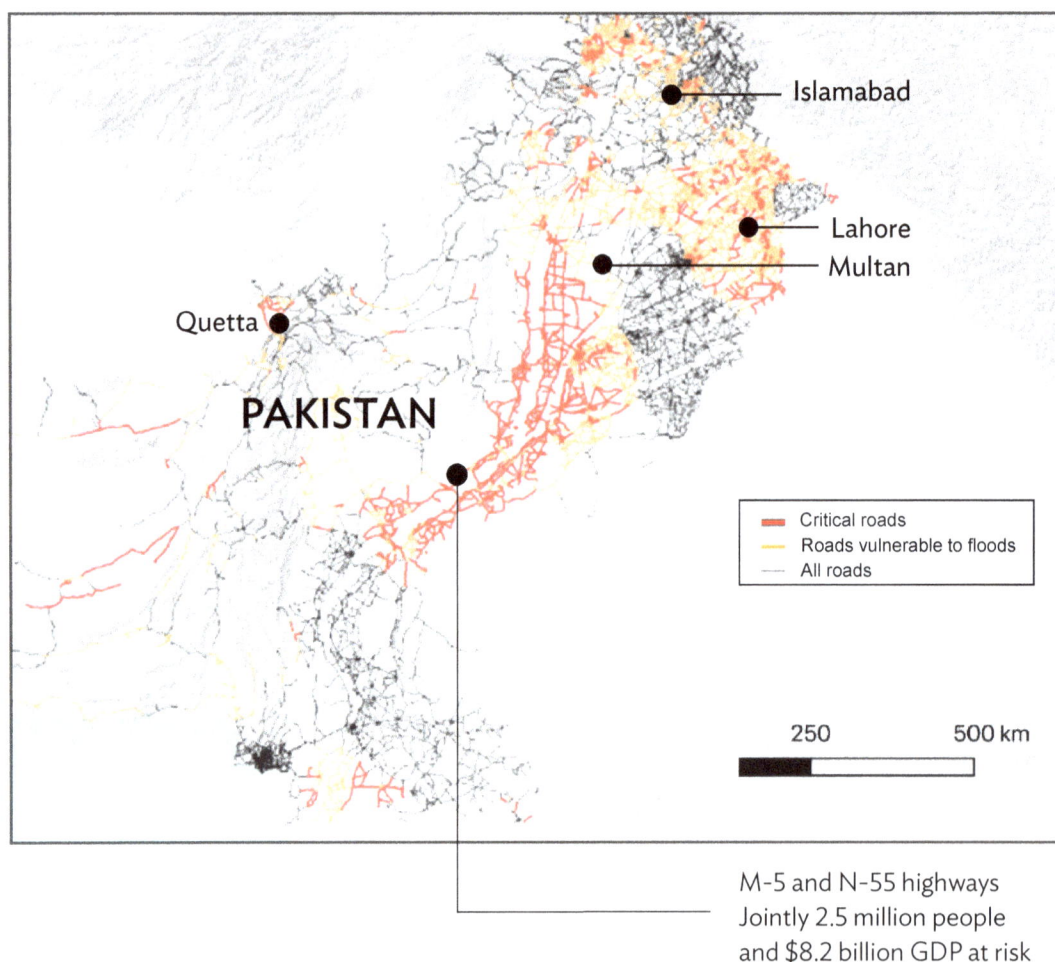

- Islamabad
- Lahore
- Multan
- Quetta

PAKISTAN

Legend:
- Critical roads
- Roads vulnerable to floods
- All roads

250   500 km

M-5 and N-55 highways
Jointly 2.5 million people
and $8.2 billion GDP at risk

GDP = gross domestic product.
Note: The map highlights road segments used in the analysis which are not intended to represent geopolitical boundaries.
Source: Vivid Economics.

- **Step 5:** Assess future changes in risk.
  - Scenarios that take climate and socioeconomic uncertainty into account can be created to understand better how risk is likely to evolve in the future. Projections of socioeconomic and climate uncertainty according to specific scenarios can be used in considering a range of possible future levels of risk. The IPCC has developed universally recognized scenarios, which can be downscaled to the local level and overlaid with present-day risk assessments. Tools exist to help decision makers plan interventions over time, given the uncertainties. Among these tools is the dynamic adaptive policy pathways (DAPP) approach, which is applied in this report to embankment-raising interventions in Cambodia (in Section 5.5 and the Appendix).

A number of key lessons emerge from the assessment of critical roads and earthquake risk in Pakistan:

- The foregoing analysis indicates that 35.5 million people in the country are at risk from earthquakes that prevent access to key services, and regions served by roads at risk from earthquakes account for 16.6% of Pakistan's GDP. Overall, the estimates show that $16.5 million in investment in seismic road resilience would be needed to lessen this risk. Complementary disaster risk management measures could then be applied to manage residual risks that cannot be effectively reduced.

- Open-source data can deliver deep risk insights. Data from several sources can be combined to allow the analysis of different dimensions of risk.

- Tailoring the analysis to policy priorities ensures that the risk assessment effectively supports decision-making.

- Using simple metrics is a powerful approach to risk assessment and communication, particularly in data- or capacity-scarce environments.

- The criticality assessment method presented here is widely replicable, thanks to the availability of open-source data.

- Once critical assets within the road network have been successfully identified, location-specific analysis can be done to complement the countrywide risk assessments, as illustrated in this example, and further inform investment decisions regarding critical parts of the network.

5 Prioritizing Infrastructure Resilience Investments

5.1 Overview

Once risks are understood, authorities can decide what investments they need to make to promote resilience. Investing in infrastructure resilience before a disaster occurs can reduce costly damage and losses in the event of a disaster and provide additional benefits.

This section deals mainly with identifying, prioritizing, and effectively combining investments to reduce risk (see Figure 12). Investments form a subset of the full range of resilience solutions, alongside operational changes (see Section 6) and risk transfer options (Section 7).

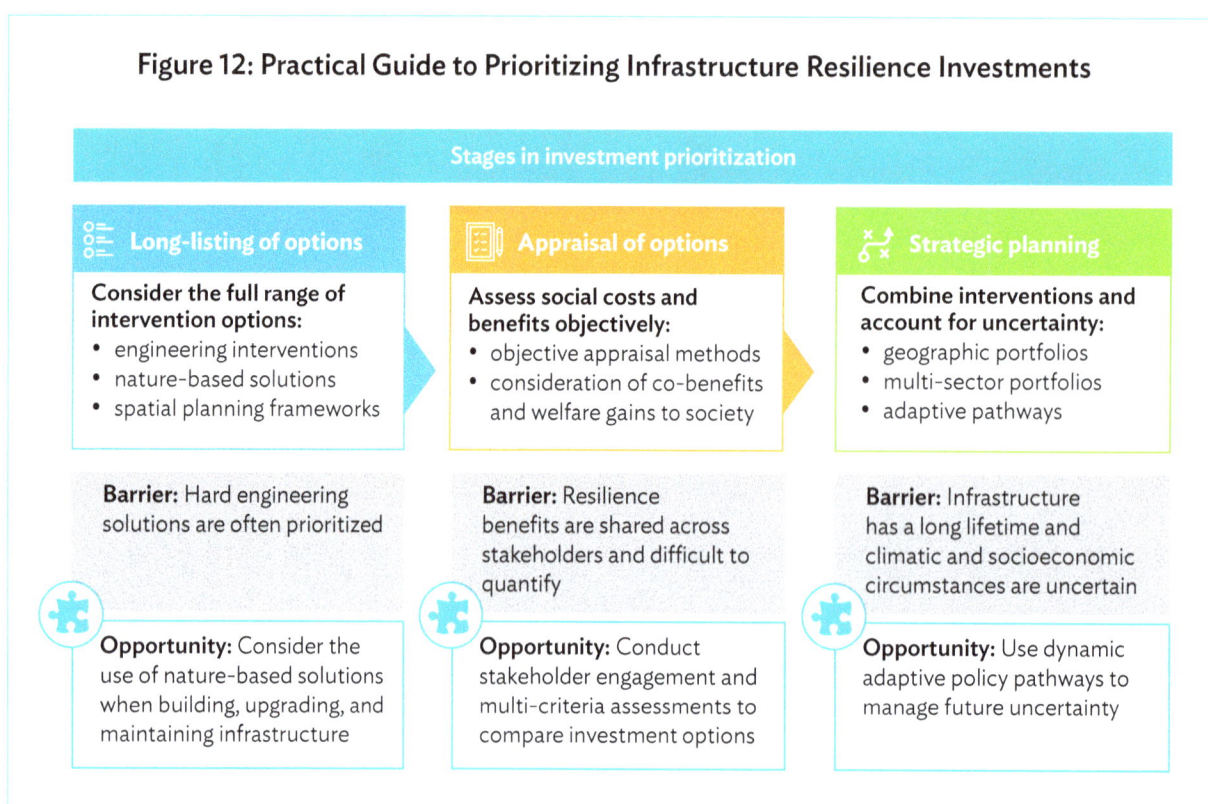

Figure 12: Practical Guide to Prioritizing Infrastructure Resilience Investments

Stages in investment prioritization		
Long-listing of options	**Appraisal of options**	**Strategic planning**
Consider the full range of intervention options: • engineering interventions • nature-based solutions • spatial planning frameworks	Assess social costs and benefits objectively: • objective appraisal methods • consideration of co-benefits and welfare gains to society	Combine interventions and account for uncertainty: • geographic portfolios • multi-sector portfolios • adaptive pathways
Barrier: Hard engineering solutions are often prioritized	**Barrier:** Resilience benefits are shared across stakeholders and difficult to quantify	**Barrier:** Infrastructure has a long lifetime and climatic and socioeconomic circumstances are uncertain
Opportunity: Consider the use of nature-based solutions when building, upgrading, and maintaining infrastructure	**Opportunity:** Conduct stakeholder engagement and multi-criteria assessments to compare investment options	**Opportunity:** Use dynamic adaptive policy pathways to manage future uncertainty

Source: Vivid Economics.

Long-listing of options

Infrastructure resilience can be achieved through a variety of engineered and nature-based approaches. Nature-based solution (NBS) approaches are ways of protecting, managing, enhancing, or restoring natural ecosystems to support infrastructure resilience. Engineered approaches, on the other hand, involve investments in gray infrastructure (traditional man-made structures). Engineered approaches are typically employed to improve infrastructure resilience, but NBS and other alternative interventions can be cheaper, have fewer negative externalities, and provide additional benefits, some of which are realized regardless of the type of disaster that occurs (Chausson et al. 2020; NBSI 2018; Seddon et al. 2020). There is growing evidence that for mild or less extreme hazards, NBS approaches are more cost-effective than traditional engineering approaches. Moreover, NBS approaches can be resource-efficient and can play a key role in transitioning to a less resource-intensive growth model (Sowińska-Świerkosz and García 2021). They also provide flexibility in responding to changing circumstances and avoid lock-in into specific pathways. NBS approaches can be implemented in combination with traditional engineering approaches to manage physical constraints, such as lack of space in urban settings, using complementarities between the two approaches to good advantage.

Risk-informed spatial planning offers opportunities for resilience by locating infrastructure assets in areas that are less exposed to natural hazards. When designing infrastructure service expansions, it is important to consider where the infrastructure assets will be located. Hazard footprints may change in the future, and an area that currently appears to be at low risk may become exposed to hazards over the lifetime of the assets. Planning for these changes, for example, by ensuring that transport routes skirt areas at high risk of future flooding, can avoid the high costs of reinforcement and protection later on. Places where people and businesses are likely to relocate, in response to large-scale infrastructure investments, must also be taken into account, and safe settlement patterns, away from high-risk areas, ensured. Various development control regulations can then be put in place through spatial planning to support the resilience of future investments, as highlighted in the example of coastal infrastructure planning in Viet Nam in Box 6.

Box 6: Alternative Interventions for Infrastructure Resilience in Viet Nam

In Viet Nam, provincial governments have integrated climate risk into coastal infrastructure planning with the support of the United Nations Development Programme (UNDP) and the Asian Development Bank. Coastal development policies have been updated, climate-proof design codes developed for coastal infrastructure, and policy-makers trained to integrate climate knowledge into infrastructure planning.

A regulatory basis for consistent spatial planning of future investments, through in-depth assessment of climate change impact on relevant regions, and a technical capacity-building program for decision makers have been established. Government standards and specifications for rural infrastructure have also been updated to include broader environmental considerations and allow the procurement of a wider range of resilience solutions. The ability of provincial governments to set out a long list of investment options has improved as a result.

Source: UNDP (n.d.).

Risk-informed planning can be supported by development partners. In Tonga, for instance, ADB identified and mapped out key assets against current and future climate risks across Tongatapu (see Box 7). The assessment was made to identify opportunities to increase resilience in hazard-prone areas, and direct investments toward safer areas. This example brings out the value of risk-informed spatial planning in helping to steer development in a resilient direction.

Box 7: Multi-hazard Climate and Disaster Risk Assessment in Tonga

The Kingdom of Tonga is among the most hazard-exposed countries in the world. Many of its infrastructure assets are at risk of the impact of natural hazards.

In 2020, the Government of Tonga and the Asian Development Bank carried out the Multi-Hazard Climate and Disaster Risk Assessment Project. The infrastructure assets of Tongatapu, the main island, were mapped against various natural hazards. A risk index was developed and towns were ranked against single- and multi-hazard threats. The assessment covered the following aspects:

- infrastructure assets (roads, power and water assets, and buildings); and
- natural hazards (earthquakes, windstorms, tsunamis, rainfed and coastal flooding, and sea level rise under different climate scenarios).

This risk assessment was a crucial step in designing and operating resilient infrastructure assets in the context of various disaster types in Tonga. The risk index informs developers of the required stringency of resilience measures, and of the hazards at which these measures should be targeted. Moreover, relatively safe zones were identified as potential locations for infrastructure assets, supporting the government in steering new investments away from the most hazard-exposed areas.

Source: ADB (2021a).

Zoning can be an effective mechanism for enforcing risk-informed spatial planning. Stakeholders in the focus group meetings recognized the fact that zoning is currently applied unequally across sectors and countries, and that better, more consistent zoning is needed to improve investment decisions. In Indonesia, stakeholders described how the national spatial planning law, passed by national, state, and local governments, guides infrastructure investments. If a road has to be repaired after a disaster, its location—in a red, amber, or green zone—is assessed to determine which resilience requirements apply. Stringent resilience requirements apply in the red zone. In the amber zone, road construction or retrofitting in the disaster-affected areas must be done together with some interventions. In the green zone, on the other hand, roads can be constructed or retrofitted according to normal standards. This assessment was applied in post-disaster recovery efforts in Central Sulawesi in 2018.

Appraisal of options

To ensure that investment is allocated where it can have the most impact, the costs and benefits of intervention options can be compared. The categories of benefits and costs to be considered can be aligned with the objectives defined in the Triple Dividend framework (see Section 2), to cover avoided damage and losses, unlocked economic potential, and development co-benefits associated with the proposed infrastructure investment. The use of cost–benefit analysis to determine resilience options varies across the DMCs. In Fiji, stakeholders across various sectors indicated that cost–benefit analyses were indeed often used to compare investment options, with support from external regional organizations like the Pacific Community. In other instances, however, stakeholders noted that investment decisions were often made ad hoc, instead of relying on standardized appraisal mechanisms.

Investment decisions do not always rely on strategic assessments and may not take socioeconomic benefits into account. In focus group meetings, stakeholders emphasized the importance of including social costs and benefits in appraisal frameworks. But the discussions suggested that appraisal mechanisms do not sufficiently consider socioeconomic variables, especially for vulnerable groups. The appraisal is narrowly focused on return on investment, without considering societal and other benefits and co-benefits.

As benefits are shared across a variety of stakeholders, effective engagement is needed to ensure that these are fully understood by decision makers. Stakeholder survey results showed the inadequacy of current information dissemination and exchange in efficiently identifying the resulting benefits to the various stakeholders, and prioritizing investments accordingly. Limited capacity for research and the collection of new data was also indicated as a key barrier to the careful consideration of the range of stakeholder benefits in cost–benefit assessments.

Strategic planning

A comprehensive resilience strategy combines individual interventions to promote system-wide resilience. Geographic portfolios coordinate interventions across space. Where hazards are confined to specific areas, these portfolios can be highly effective, as flood risk management portfolios like the Delta Programme in the Netherlands and the Thames 2100 plan in the United Kingdom have demonstrated (Delta Programme Commissioner, Netherlands, 2018; Environment Agency, United Kingdom, 2012). Multi-sectoral portfolios coordinate interventions across sectors and can leverage the positive spillover effects of interventions across interdependent infrastructure networks. But they require cross-sectoral planning and decision-making.

Flexible approaches can improve decision-making when future climate and socioeconomic circumstances are uncertain. Infrastructure assets have a long lifetime, and irreversible decisions about how they should be configured can lead to maladaptation over the long term. Flexible approaches that allow systems to adapt to changing circumstances can reduce this problem. The adaptive pathway approach, for example, allows decision makers to change course by setting out sequenced investment actions. This approach is discussed in Opportunity 8.

Box 8: Geographic Portfolios in the Mekong Delta

The geographic portfolio of mitigation and adaptation options for flood control across the Mekong Delta incorporates an adaptive strategy for the period until 2100, outlining "no-regret," "priority," and "structural" options that can be implemented, depending on future climatic and socioeconomic trends. The Mekong Delta Plan of 2013 proposes the coordination of flood risk management measures across the entire Upper Delta, for agriculture development as well as flood control. Complementing local aquaculture with nature-based solutions, by using the generated effluent to nourish reforested mangroves, is also recommended.

Source: MONRE and MARD, Viet Nam, and Government of the Netherlands (2013).

The stakeholder survey conducted for this report brought out the fact that decision makers are typically more familiar with engineered investments than with alternative interventions. Respondents noted that solutions other than hard engineering infrastructure are often left out of appraisal processes, even though their importance is recognized. Bearing out this finding, over 80% of respondents have implemented physical protective infrastructure and over 60% have invested in physical upgrades and reinforcements, as shown in Figure 13. In comparison, less than half have invested in nature-based solutions.

Figure 13: Survey Results on Existing Resilient Investment Options

SURVEY QUESTION: Over the last five years, which of the following interventions have been undertaken to improve infrastructure resilience in your country and sector?

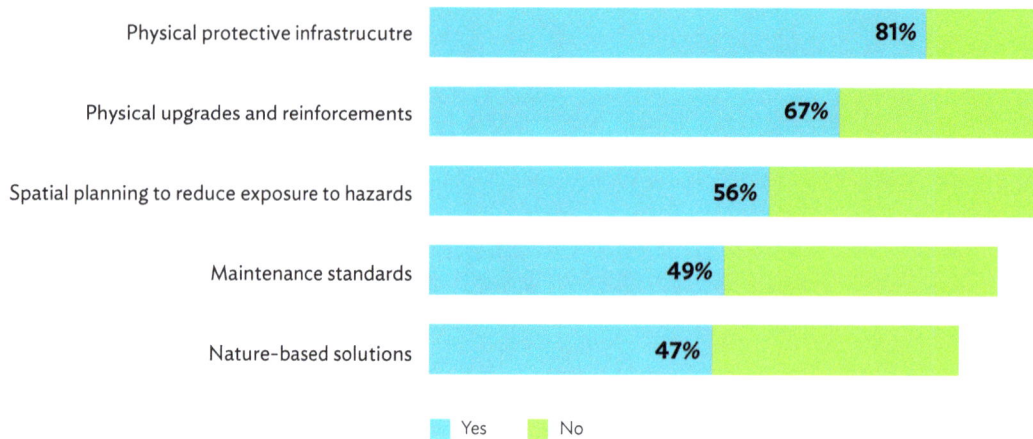

	Yes	No
Physical protective infrastrucutre	81%	
Physical upgrades and reinforcements	67%	
Spatial planning to reduce exposure to hazards	56%	
Maintenance standards	49%	
Nature-based solutions	47%	

Source: Vivid Economics, based on data from stakeholder survey.

Survey respondents singled out the following priorities in overcoming key barriers and improving investment prioritization:

- **Better sharing of examples and best practices from other countries and sectors.** Given the generally limited experience in many parts of the region, especially in innovative approaches like nature-based solutions (see Opportunity 6), sharing knowledge and peer learning has significant potential to accelerate adoption. Knowledge about the adaptation of best practices to local contexts was also an identified requirement among several respondents.

- **Simple and inclusive appraisal methods.** As pointed out earlier, decisions are often made in data-scarce environments, and could affect a wide range of groups. The full social costs and benefits of investment options can be determined through inclusive multi-criteria assessment (see Opportunity 7 and Opportunity 8).

- **Coordination mechanisms across geographies and sectors.** Coordinating investments across a wide range stakeholders is challenging. Mechanisms that will facilitate communication and joint decision-making are needed to improve the impact of resilience investments throughout the infrastructure system (see Opportunity 16 in Section 8).

5.2   Opportunity 6: Consider the Use of Nature-Based Solutions when Building, Upgrading, and Maintaining Infrastructure

Nature-based solutions can be cheaper and more sustainable than engineered solutions and can offer co-benefits to local communities. They can unlock economic potential by strengthening the resilience of local livelihoods, supporting local economic development, and (often) developing tourism potential. They also deliver co-benefits by improving biodiversity, air quality, opportunities for recreation and physical activity, and general well-being (Griscom et al. 2017; Browder et al. 2019). NBS approaches can also create synergies between climate mitigation and social and ecological outcomes. These approaches are often at least as effective as other options for making the impact of climate change less severe, according to the literature. The evidence and worked examples are, however, centered on the Global North[5] (Chausson et al. 2020). For instance, coastal defenses in the United States, using NBS approaches, were estimated to be two to five times more effective than their engineering counterparts in high water depth and at lower wave heights (Narayan et al. 2016, quoted in Seddon et al. 2020). These approaches therefore present a key option for the DMCs to consider when designing infrastructure plans, including plans for upgrading existing infrastructure.

The manifold benefits require coordination across relevant stakeholders. Coordination from an early stage of planning can ensure that the role of ecosystem services in local communities is fully understood, and that mechanisms for protecting or enhancing the services are sustainable. Legal frameworks and incentive structures like payments for ecosystem services (PES) programs can formalize cooperation.

The benefits of nature-based solutions have so far been demonstrated most clearly with respect to managing water-related risks. For example, in the Philippines, mangroves, reefs, and other natural systems prevent more than $1 billion in disaster losses each year (Tercek 2017).

In Fiji, nature-based solutions form part of disaster preparedness. According to stakeholder discussions, mangrove plantations have been developed along the coastline to protect road infrastructure and surrounding villages from tidal waves and coastal erosion. The mangrove project is supported by the Department of Environment (under the Ministry of Local Government, Urban Development, Housing and Environment), international organizations, and local authorities and community groups.

Table 4 provides an overview of practical applications of nature-based solutions, as replacements or enhancements of engineered solutions.

Table 4: Examples of Nature-Based Solutions Implemented to Replace or Enhance Engineered Solutions

Challenge	Engineered Solutions	Nature-Based Solutions	Integrated Examples
Urban stormwater and flood management	• Retrofitted/Enhanced urban stormwater drainage systems • Engineered flood protection	• Green roofs • Urban gardens and green spaces • Riparian and wetland vegetation restoration, creation, and management	• Uptake of green roofs, bioswales, and rain gardens to regulate stormwater runoff and reduce flows to drainage system
Extreme (urban) heat	• Cooling centers and air-conditioning • Spray decks • Pools • Misting systems • Shading devices	• Green roofs • Urban gardens and green spaces • Street trees	• Green roofs, bioswales, and rain gardens providing cooling through evapotranspiration and reduction of urban heat island effect
Coastal flooding, storm surge, sea level rise, and erosion	• Seawalls, dikes, permanent artificial walls, and temporary storm barriers • Improved drainage systems	• Conservation, management, restoration, or creation of the following: – Coral reefs (including the use of artificial substrate) – Oyster reefs – Seagrass – Coastal wetlands, mangroves, and salt marshes – Sand dunes and beaches	• Restoration/Conservation of mangrove belts that support sea dikes as a first line of defense to reduce flood risk and erosion

continued on next page

---

[5] The Global North can be defined as the ensemble of most industrialized and developed countries, located in majority in the Northern hemisphere.

Table 4 continued

Challenge	Engineered Solutions	Nature-Based Solutions	Integrated Examples
Inland flooding	• Alluvial dikes and dams (creation, retrofitting, and maintenance) • Improved pumping, piping, and storage systems	• Upstream vegetation management • Forest restoration • Riparian and wetland restoration/ creation and management, living weirs, and check dams • Floodplain management	• Forest restoration around alluvial dikes and dams
Landslides	• Retaining walls • Gabions	• Upslope vegetation management • Reforestation and afforestation	• Upslope vegetation strengthening the resilience of retaining walls
Water scarcity	• Reservoirs/Dams • Concrete catchments • Aqueducts • Desalination plants (coastal)	• Watershed restoration, including reforestation or afforestation • Permeable "green" areas for groundwater replenishment	• Watershed restoration around dams to regulate water supply and decrease erosion and sedimentation
Soil erosion and sedimentation	• Retaining walls • Terracing • Dredging programs	• Upslope vegetation restoration and management • Reforestation and, where appropriate, afforestation • Management of littoral vegetation and wetlands	

Source: Silva Zuñiga et al. (2020).

Several considerations related to different types of nature-based solutions affect their applicability across DMCs. Different NBS types may be more applicable than others for specific use cases across DMCs. Indeed, certain types, such as reforestation or wetland restoration, require a large amount of land, which can be challenging in urban settings, where other options, such as green roofs, can prove to be more appropriate (see example in Box 9). Moreover, some outstanding challenges apply across most NBS types. For instance, existing frameworks for infrastructure implementation and monitoring must be adapted to suit nature-based solutions, and valuation models can be more complex for these types of solutions than for engineering solutions (Nelson et al. 2020). More systematic consideration of NBS approaches in investment decisions and sharing of success stories will be important in overcoming these barriers.

Box 9: Urban Flood Management in the People's Republic of China

In response to major storms damaging infrastructure and causing flooding with severe humanitarian and economic impact, the People's Republic of China (PRC) has invested $300 billion in urban flood management strategies for Beijing, Shanghai, Shenzhen, and Wuhan. These "sponge cities" use green and blue infrastructure, such as permeable pavement, rain gardens (as catchment basins), and wetlands (as buffers against floodwater). By 2030, if the government's plans are realized, sponge city projects will have been installed in 80% of the country's urban areas.

The Asian Development Bank has supported some of these developments, by providing a $150 million loan for the improvement of water management in Jiangxi province and Pingxiang city. River wetlands and floodplains were rehabilitated to enhance flood control capacity. Green urban infrastructure, such as green roofs, rain gardens, and porous pavements, was installed to reduce surface runoff. As a result, a 1-in-20-year flood control standard was achieved.

Sources: Roxburgh (2017); ADB (2015); and Ohshita and Johnson (2017), quoted in World Bank (2018).

5.3 Opportunity 7: Conduct Stakeholder Engagement and Multi-criteria Assessments to Compare Investment Options

Benefits of infrastructure resilience interventions are shared across a variety of stakeholders and cannot always be quantified. A coordinated and inclusive approach that considers both qualitative and quantitative evidence when comparing investment options is required.

To improve the resilience of infrastructure services, private developers, key economic sectors, and the engineering community must be engaged in the effort, according to focus group discussions. For example, in Fiji and in many other parts of the Pacific, tourism is an important economic sector, requiring tourism infrastructure, as well as transport, communication, water, and energy infrastructure. Planned infrastructure resilience measures will have to be discussed with companies in the sector to ensure that the measures provide co-benefits and do not create unintended negative consequences.

Multi-criteria assessments engage key stakeholders in the joint evaluation of investment options and the identification of options that offer the highest benefits. The Department for Environment, Food and Rural Affairs in the United Kingdom proposes a five-step approach to multi-criteria assessments, shown in Figure 14.

Figure 14: Five-Step Approach to Integrating Nonmonetary Evidence into Valuation and Appraisal

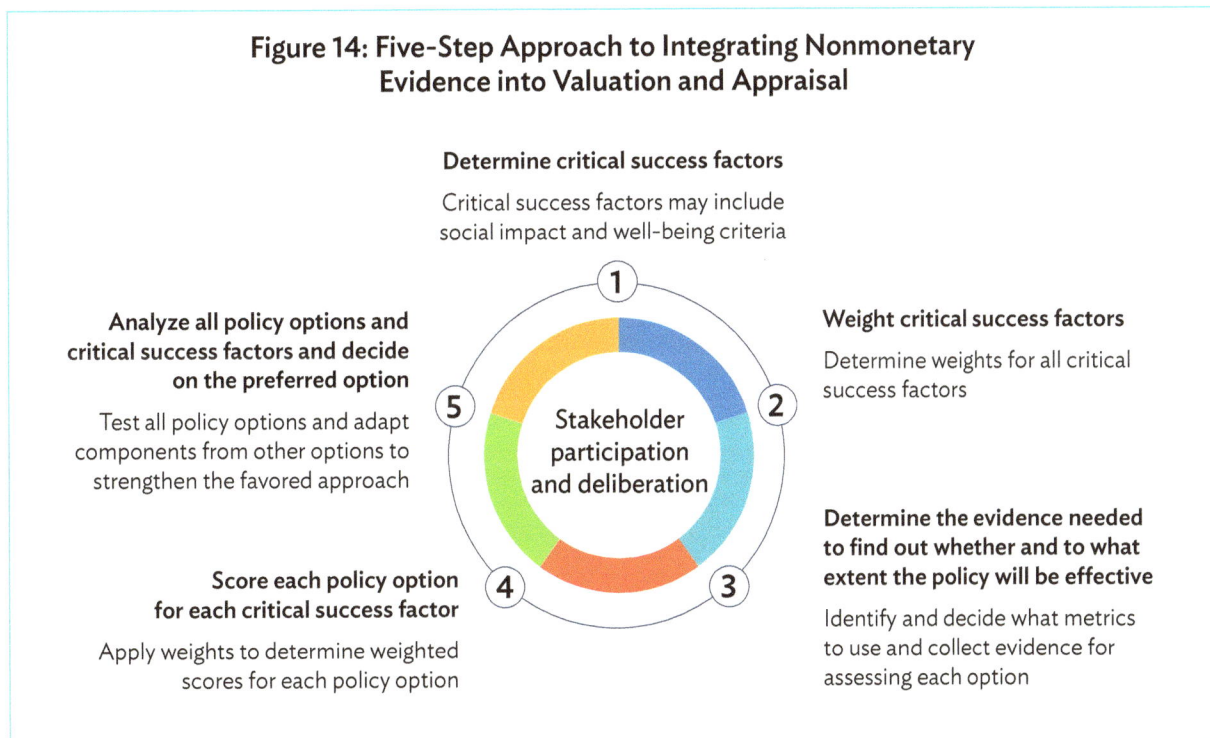

Determine critical success factors

Critical success factors may include social impact and well-being criteria

1

Weight critical success factors

Determine weights for all critical success factors

2

Analyze all policy options and critical success factors and decide on the preferred option

Test all policy options and adapt components from other options to strengthen the favored approach

5

Stakeholder participation and deliberation

Determine the evidence needed to find out whether and to what extent the policy will be effective

Identify and decide what metrics to use and collect evidence for assessing each option

3

Score each policy option for each critical success factor

Apply weights to determine weighted scores for each policy option

4

Source: Maxwell et al. (2011), adapted by Vivid Economics.

- **Steps 1–2:** Assess critical success factors and their relative importance, using the Triple Dividend framework introduced in Section 2 (see Table 5). Focus group discussions and joint working groups between sector ministries, infrastructure operators, local authorities, and community representatives can be helpful in determining the types of costs and benefits to count and the stakeholders that will incur the costs or derive the benefits.

- **Step 3:** Translate the jointly agreed costs and benefits into comparable metrics and collect evidence for assessing each option. The metrics can be quantitative, where possible (see Table 6, for example), but qualitative metrics can be equally decision-relevant.

- **Steps 4–5:** Finally, score the options, and involve key stakeholders in selecting the winners. Identifying complementary interventions to strengthen the outcomes leads to more effective resilience strategies.

Table 5: Costs and Benefits to Consider when Appraising Investment Options

	Items	Details
Costs	Up-front investment	Investment costs, and costs of financing (if applicable) Training and capacity-building costs
	Ongoing costs	Changes in maintenance and operating costs resulting from the investment Negative impact on ecosystem services or livelihoods
	Loss of economic potential	Reduced availability of resources for other productive investments because of additional costs (compared with business as usual)
	Development co-costs	Reduced access to amenities Degradation of the natural environment
Benefits	Avoided damage and losses	Reduced number of people affected by infrastructure failure, and avoided or reduced fatalities Avoided or reduced damage to infrastructure and other strategic assets Avoided or reduced economic losses from disruptions to infrastructure service delivery Avoided risk of cascading impact for the wider infrastructure system, and the implications of such impact for people and the economy
	Unlocked economic potential	Economic stimulus from the investment Investments in productive assets encouraged by reduced risk profile
	Development co-benefits	Protected or enhanced ecosystem services Support for local livelihoods

Source: Vivid Economics.

Table 6 presents examples of quantifying methods for estimating the number of people affected by infrastructure failure due to floods. Energy, water, transport, communications, and urban infrastructure networks are considered here. The triggering hazards can be fluvial, pluvial, or coastal floods, caused by snow melt, excessive rainfall, cyclones, or tsunamis.

Table 6: Ways of Quantifying the Reduction in the Number of People Affected by Infrastructure Failure, and Flood Fatality Avoidance or Reduction—Examples

Quantification Output	Quantification Methodology Steps and Options
Number of injuries and fatalities averted	• Estimate the average annual injuries and fatalities in the evacuation shelter catchment area. The estimates could be based on historical data, assumptions, or survey data. EM-DAT,[a] an international database of emergency events, may provide relevant historical information. • Estimate injuries and fatalities averted per shelter. The estimates could be based on a historical comparison of areas with and without access to shelters (adjusting for local factors and flood levels, where possible). They could also be based on simplifying assumptions using historical data or academic literature, such as the probability of injury/fatality. For example, a comparative analysis of different types of flood shelters in Bangladesh conducted by the Institute of Water and Flood Management, the Bangladesh University of Engineering and Technology (BUET), and BRAC University provides a comparison of the structures of different types of shelters that could form the basis for assumptions.[b] • To apply these estimates to new shelters, scale the injuries/fatalities averted and adjust the figures by the number of people gaining access to shelters, the likely flood depth under different scenarios, and other local conditions.
Number of people requiring short-term humanitarian assistance averted	• Estimate the population exposed to flooding in the catchment area of the infrastructure, using the exposure data. • Estimate the proportion of the population requiring relief. The proportion of population requiring assistance under different flood depth scenarios or based on historical data can be estimated. The international emergency events database EM-DAT may provide relevant historical information. • Estimate the proportion of the population not needing assistance because of their access to resilient infrastructure. This estimate could be based on a historical comparison of areas, the flood impact on resilient versus non-resilient infrastructure in place, and the number of people affected under each scenario. This comparison can support estimates of the exposed proportion of the population within a catchment area of infrastructure.
Length of disruption to critical infrastructure services	• Estimate the population exposed to flooding in the catchment area of infrastructure, using the exposure data. • Estimate the duration of flooding and the corresponding length of disruption to businesses and services. The Dartmouth Flood Observatory[c] archive of large flood events can be used in assessing the historical duration of flood events and estimating an average annual event. An additional buffer for recovery time may have to be added, as services may be disrupted beyond the duration of the hazard event. • Estimate the proportion of the population with sustained access to key services because of their access to resilient infrastructure. This estimate could be based on a historical comparison of areas, survey data showing how people make use of resilient infrastructure (to inform assumptions), or estimates of the exposed proportion of the population within a catchment area of infrastructure.

[a] CRED (n.d.).   [b] Mallick et al. (2010).   [c] DFO, University of Colorado, USA (n.d.).

Source: Vivid Economics, for World Bank (2021).

5.4 Opportunity 8: Use Dynamic Adaptive Policy Pathways to Manage Future Uncertainty

Uncertainty around future risks makes investment planning for infrastructure resilience a challenge. Infrastructure assets are durable, long-lived, and often economically important investments. Climate and socioeconomic circumstances could change over their lifetime. If decisions made regarding the configuration of infrastructure systems are irreversible, maladaptation could result over the long term. Building infrastructure resilience can be high-cost, but maladapted infrastructure can be even more costly to economies and societies. Flexible approaches that allow systems to adapt to future circumstances can reduce this problem.

The dynamic adaptive policy pathways (DAPP) approach can help decision makers manage future uncertainty. The approach explicitly involves decision-making over time. It is proactive, dynamic, and flexible in responding to how the future actually unfolds. Investment actions are set out in a sequenced manner. Lower-cost and smaller investment actions are typically chosen in the short term, even as a framework of potential future actions is also built. Through continuous monitoring, significant changes in climate science, growth projections, technology, and other aspects of the local environment that weaken resilience and call for a reassessment of uncertainties and actions are identified. Decision makers can then modify their investment strategies to suit the changes, thus reducing the risk of locking in maladaptation. The approach is most useful where uncertainty is high and there is a marked variation in the outcomes of the choices that decision makers face (Haasnoot et al. 2013).

Low-regret actions are taken in the short-term, while further research is conducted to inform future decisions, which allows use of new technology and research. Low-regret actions designate low-cost actions likely to provide large benefits under current climate change scenarios. Decision points, where new information is reviewed, resilience standards are assessed, and strategies are adjusted, are defined. New technology and research can be used to full advantage as it emerges across the future decision points.

Figure 15 illustrates this approach. The blue circles in the chart are decision points at which the next step is decided on and implemented with the aim of staying within the adaptive—or in this case, resilient—space. An example showing the application of the DAPP approach to the planning of an airport in the Cook Islands can be found in Box 10.

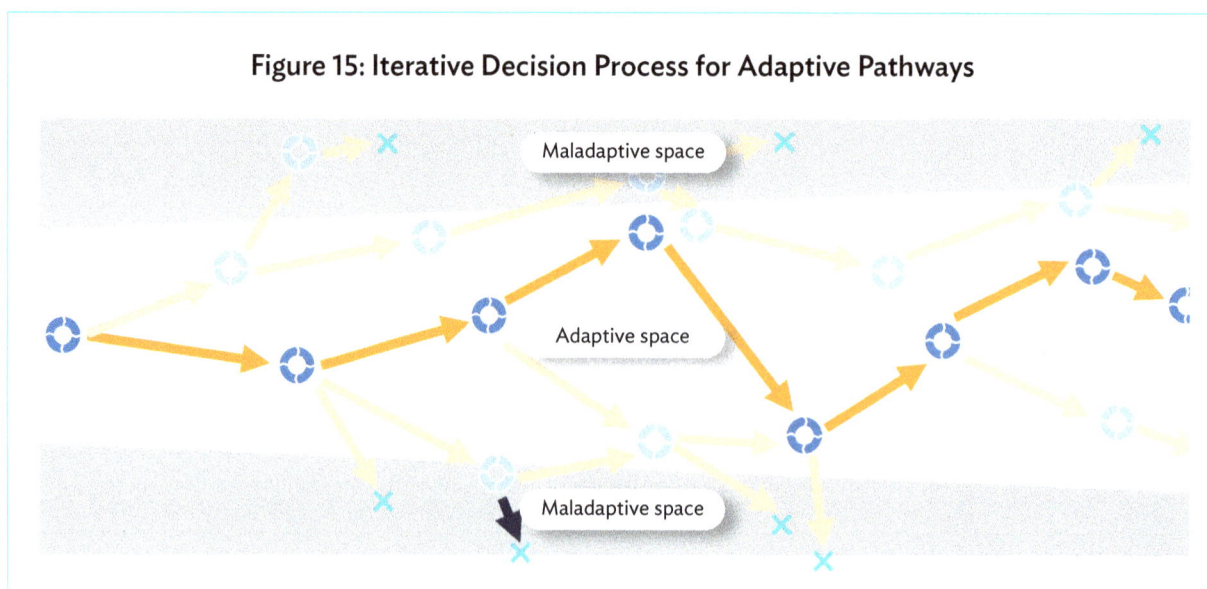

Figure 15: Iterative Decision Process for Adaptive Pathways

Source: Wise et al. (2014).

So far, adaptive pathways have mostly been applied at a relatively small spatial scale rather than at a national or multistate level (Moss and Martin 2012). In the next subsection is a case study prepared for this report, giving details of how adaptive pathways can be developed to promote flood resilience in Cambodia.

5.5 Application: Decision-Making under Uncertainty—Dynamic Adaptive Policy Pathways for Flood Risk Reduction Investments in Cambodia

This case study assesses the potential for the DAPP approach to inform flood risk investments in key road segments in Cambodia.[6] It explores different embankment options for making roads more resilient to floods, in order to demonstrate the potential benefits of early resilience action. A variety of flood risk mitigation and resilience-building measures other than embankment raising exist (e.g., smart monitoring, enhanced surface treatment, and nature-based solutions). These measures are beyond the scope of the study, but they can form part of a holistic approach to flood risk management, with or without DAPP.

Building road resilience in Cambodia is critical to maintaining economic activity but made challenging by climate and socioeconomic uncertainty. The government currently assesses flood risk using an in-house tool to meet set resilience objectives, and enhanced risk information could improve decision-making. Exploring the potential for dynamic adaptive pathways is therefore particularly relevant in this context.

Policy-makers can follow three main steps when developing these pathways: (i) objective setting and long-listing, (ii) appraisal of options, and (iii) strategic planning. These steps are discussed below.

Objective setting and long-listing

The objectives of the DAPP inform the list of interventions considered. The objectives that need to be defined include the asset to be protected, the hazards to which the asset is vulnerable, the spatial and temporal unit of analysis, the relevant dimensions of uncertainty, the resilience objective for the asset, and other policy priorities.

- **Here, the analysis is focused on roads and their vulnerability to floods.** The analysis is performed for the following years: 2020, 2030, 2050, and 2080. Two scenarios of climate uncertainty (Representative Concentration Pathway, or RCP, 4.5 and RCP8.5), as well as three scenarios of socioeconomic uncertainty (Shared Socioeconomic Pathway, or SSP, 1, SSP2, and SSP3), are considered.[7] These scenarios are important because the structure of the DAPP and their decision points are based on the outcomes of different scenarios.

---

[6]   Three road segments that connect the northern and southern parts of the country and thus play a key role in the circulation of goods and people were selected. The full case study, in the Appendix, contains more detailed information about the road segment selection.

[7]   The terms "Representative Concentration Pathway (RCP)" and "Shared Socioeconomic Pathway (SSP)" are defined in IPCC (2014).

- **The resilience objective is resilience to 1-in-100-year flooding.** This return period was selected on the basis of prior government risk assessments showing that it affords a reasonable level of protection, as these events are rare (MRD, Cambodia, 2018). Adjustments are made in this objective in line with climate change across the time horizon of the analysis, to maintain a fixed standard of protection for a 1-in-100-year return period even as floods become more frequent and/or severe.

- **Embankment height raising was considered as the key intervention for improving road resilience to floods.** Different embankment heights, providing protection against floods of different severity levels, are taken into account.

The options are combined to develop a map of possible intervention pathways, which describe combinations of interventions that can be deployed to meet the resilience objective. Tipping points, or thresholds at which the current levels of adaptation no longer meet resilience criteria, must first be identified. The sequence of interventions is then set so that decisions regarding adaptation interventions are made well ahead of time, to ensure that the resilience objective is always met.

The analysis indicates four sequences of actions that can protect the asset against 1-in-100-year return period flooding. The sequences are based on combinations of the following actions:

- raising the embankment to a level of protection against 1-in-100-year return period flooding (the minimum level of action required in the short term);

- raising the embankment by 0.3 meter (m) (an intermediate level of action); and/or

- raising the embankment by 1 m (the highest level of action).

Figure 16 lays out the sequence of embankment height raising against the tipping points across the two climate scenarios. According to the pathway map, any initial action taken in the short term provides protection until at least 2050, when the tipping point is reached in RCP4.5. The pathway map also shows that the outcomes diverge significantly between the climate scenarios from 2050 onward; over the long term, tipping points are reached more quickly in RCP4.5 because RCP8.5 leads to more drought-like conditions with less rainfall.

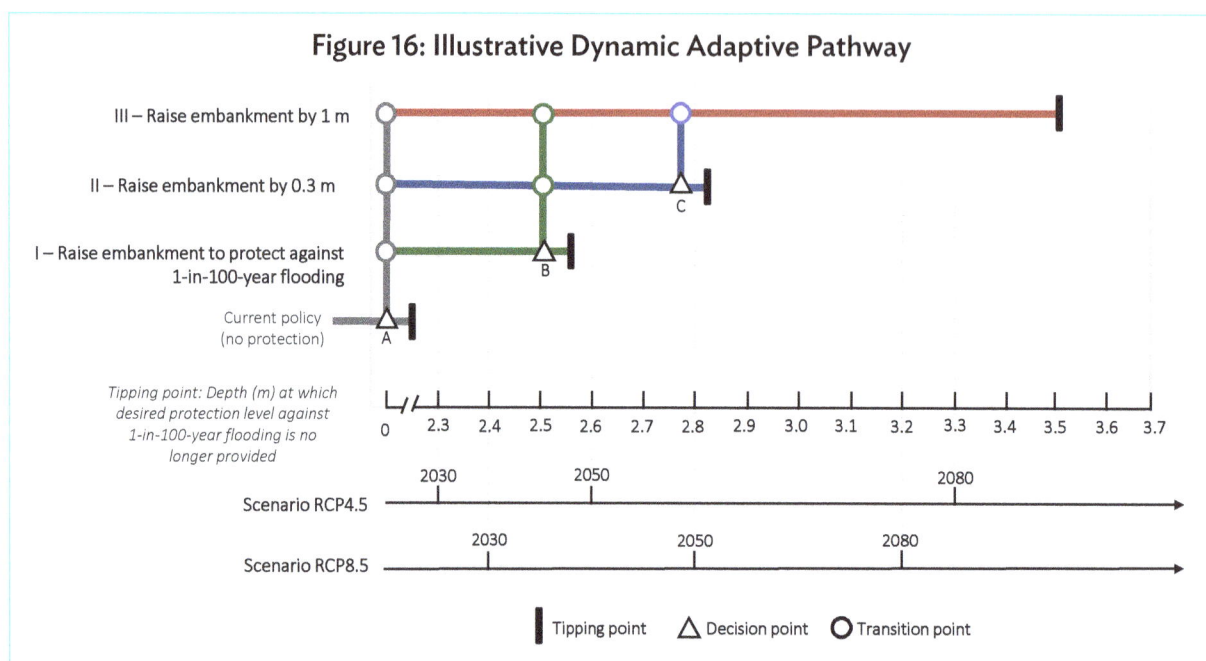

Figure 16: Illustrative Dynamic Adaptive Pathway

m = meter, RCP = Representative Concentration Pathway.

Source: Vivid Economics.

Appraisal of options

Appraisal begins by identifying the relevant costs, as well as the benefits, to consider in addition to the achievement of resilience objectives. For costs, these can include the costs of capital expenditure or labor related to the implementation of the adaptive strategy. For benefits, benefits obtained when disaster strikes (e.g., averted damage cost), as well as benefits that occur regardless, which can be economic (e.g., protecting land value) or social/environmental (e.g., improving both biodiversity and resilience), can be considered.

- For the case study scenario, the relevant cost is the capital expenditure associated with embankment raising.
- Benefits can include averted road damage, averted increase in transport time and related costs if alternative routes must be used, and additional population and GDP protected. The first-two benefits occur in the event of a disaster; the third benefit occurs regardless.

Once key costs and benefits have been identified, an assessment methodology is developed. Ideally, the methodology will monetize all costs and benefits, where possible, to standardize outcome units, quantify other outcomes where not all costs and benefits can be monetized, and make a qualitative assessment of those other outcomes.

The benefits considered in this study are averted road damage, averted traffic slowdown, and additional population and GDP protected. Global flood depth–damage functions and Cambodia-specific data on road reconstruction costs are used in estimating averted road damage. The extent of traffic disruption is based on time lost as a result of the slowdown in freight vehicles traveling over flooded, but not impassable, roads. To estimate the remaining population and GDP at risk, a spatial analysis is made of the population and GDP in areas within a given radius where road segments have been rendered impassable by flooding; the findings serve as a proxy for the population that may be unable to evacuate during extreme flooding, and for economic activity that may be unable to continue. Other factors, such as forecast lead times and early-warning capabilities, may further influence evacuation and economic activity, but have not been explicitly accounted for in the analysis. Averted road damage and traffic disruption benefits vary according to climate future; population and GDP at risk, according to socioeconomic future.

Strategic planning

An adaptive pathway based on stakeholder priorities can be selected by means of the assessment framework. The choice of pathway may vary with the categories of costs and benefits that are given priority. This prioritization can be made explicit when there are trade-offs.

Across most road segments, immediate investment in the highest level of protection is the most favorable option. Immediate high-level action reduces the investment cost considerably across road segments. For road segment 92, the investment cost for other intervention pathways is three to nine times higher, as shown in Figure 17. Monetized benefits do not vary widely across pathways. For segment 92, the monetized benefits differ by less than 10% across the different pathways, under all scenarios analyzed.

Figure 17: Investment Cost for Road Segment 92, by Pathway

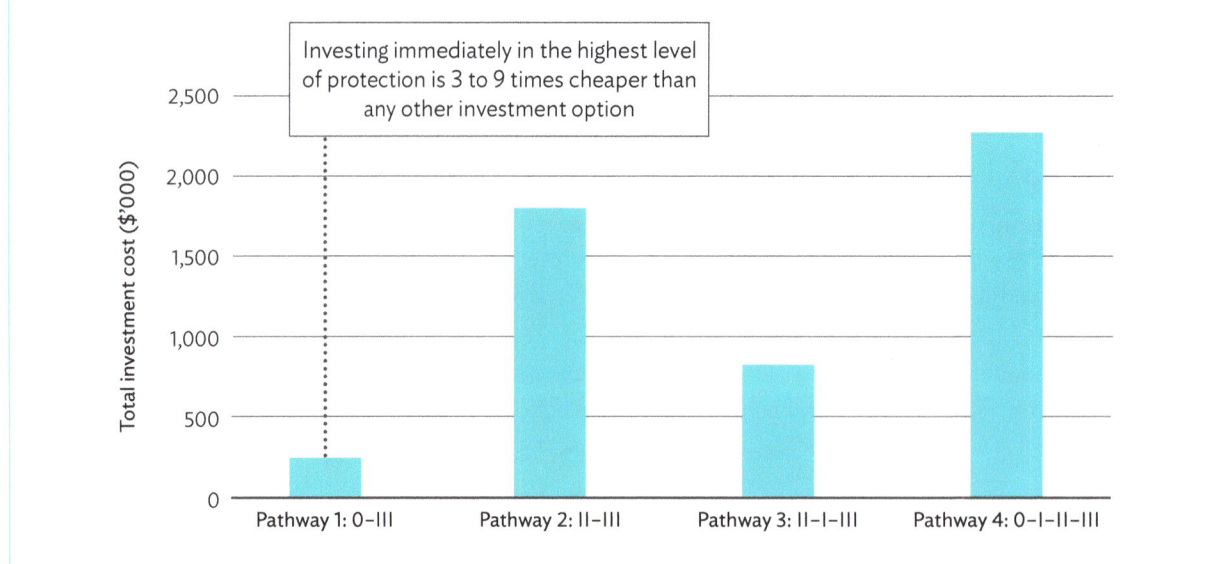

Investing immediately in the highest level of protection is 3 to 9 times cheaper than any other investment option

Total investment cost ($'000)

2,500
2,000
1,500
1,000
500
0

Pathway 1: 0–III   Pathway 2: II–III   Pathway 3: II–I–III   Pathway 4: 0–I–II–III

Source: Vivid Economics.

Pathways with incremental action, where the embankment is raised in stages, are more expensive as a whole, but may still be preferred by key stakeholders. There are only marginal differences in cost per kilometer between raising embankments to the minimum level and raising them to the maximum level. For example, for road segment 25, the total cost of investing in the lowest embankment option is only $12,000 per kilometer less than the total cost of investing in the highest embankment option, which is $1.8 million. In the long run, however, incremental pathways in this example end up being significantly more expensive overall, even when costs incurred in the future are discounted. But stakeholders may still prefer to spread the cost over time if they have competing priorities, if resources are very limited, or if the road requiring protection is very long. For other examples, there may be large dissimilarities in aggregate cost over time. In particular, where there is greater variability in future risk across the range of scenarios analyzed, the aggregate cost over time may be notably lower for incremental pathways, as the risk of early maladaptation and an associated increase in costs later on is reduced.

Across road segments, the adaptive pathway approach and multicriteria analysis highlight the importance of taking non-monetizable benefits into account. If non-monetizable benefits are not considered, appraisal using traditional tools may underestimate the investment case for resilience and affect the selection of the preferred pathway. These benefits can have long-term development implications but are more challenging to monetize.

When only the benefits from averted road damage costs and time savings from averted traffic slowdowns are considered, the assessment yields low benefit–cost ratios for most of the pathways. However, a key benefit of road resilience is maintaining road access for vulnerable populations that may require shelter during extreme events. Road infrastructure is also important for continued access to health and humanitarian services. In this case study, the pathway with immediate maximum action has the highest non-monetized benefits, as it ensures protection for as many people and as much GDP as possible. Non-monetizable benefits are assessed at the appraisal stage in this case study, but could receive greater emphasis in an approach with a different resilience objective (e.g., to minimize the population exposed to flood risk). Such an approach could determine tipping points for action based on variations in future socioeconomic conditions.

Once a pathway has been selected, it can be institutionalized with a monitoring and evaluation plan to allow the pathway to be updated as additional climate and socioeconomic risk information becomes available. Key considerations in the preparation of the monitoring and evaluation plan include the following: sensitivity of assumptions made regarding the pathways, a clear time frame for the periodic review of the selected pathway, regular updating of the plan to take new research technology and cost changes into account, and assurance that pathway actions will be implemented as sequenced. The likelihood of commitment across successive governments should also be considered, as low commitment may reduce the option value of waiting.

A deep understanding of uncertainties can lead to more cost-effective action, even when uncertainty is limited. Because of the limited variation in flood risk between climate futures, there is limited risk of maladaptation and therefore few trade-offs to resolve in achieving a high level of flood resilience in this scenario. However, the process of developing robust pathways forces decision makers to develop a comprehensive understanding of risks and uncertainties, and to prioritize resilience objectives.

A number of key findings emerge from the development of dynamic adaptive pathways for roads in Cambodia:

- **These pathways enable decision makers to take uncertainty over future climate change and socioeconomic development explicitly into account.** Variations in future risk are relatively low across the range of scenarios analyzed in the case study. In decision-making processes with a wider range of potential future outcomes, the ability to capture uncertainty becomes even more important. It is also particularly valuable in resource-constrained contexts, where reversing decisions in the future would have a greater opportunity cost.

- **The parameters and objectives of dynamic adaptive pathway development should align with policy priorities.** For instance, if non-monetizable benefits are a key focus area, policy makers can give these more weight relative to monetized benefits. In addition, the policy makers can assess the non-monetizable social or environmental benefits under different future socioeconomic conditions, to ensure that the chosen pathway is resilient to socioeconomic uncertainty.

- **In the case of embankment raising to protect roads in Cambodia, early action provides the most benefits across most road segments considered.** The marginal cost of raising roads is not high enough to counterbalance the benefits of full protection. Overall, the benefits are relatively similar across the pathways considered because climate uncertainty is limited.

6 Operating and Maintaining Infrastructure to Promote Resilience

6.1 Overview

This section considers how operation and maintenance (O&M) approaches can promote resilience before, during, and after disasters. O&M options can be considered alongside investment (Section 5) and risk transfer (Section 7) options. Figure 18 provides an overview of how O&M can support resilience before, during, and after disasters, as well as key opportunities to improve these functions.

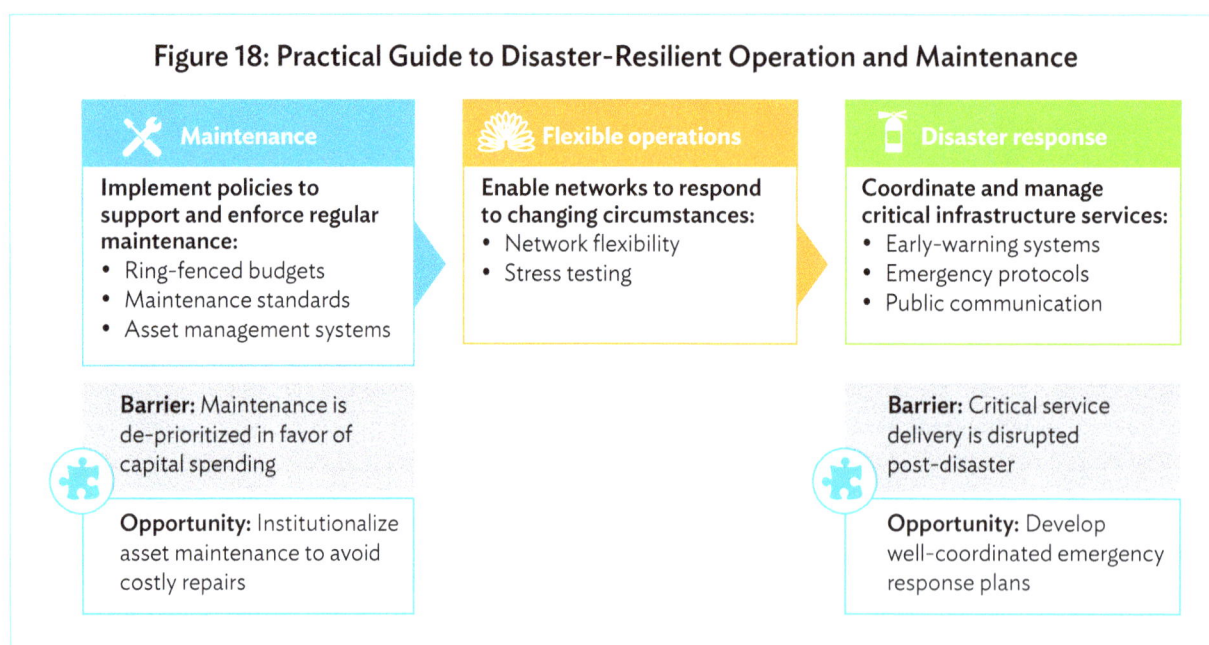

Figure 18: Practical Guide to Disaster-Resilient Operation and Maintenance

Maintenance

Implement policies to support and enforce regular maintenance:
- Ring-fenced budgets
- Maintenance standards
- Asset management systems

Flexible operations

Enable networks to respond to changing circumstances:
- Network flexibility
- Stress testing

Disaster response

Coordinate and manage critical infrastructure services:
- Early-warning systems
- Emergency protocols
- Public communication

Barrier: Maintenance is de-prioritized in favor of capital spending

Opportunity: Institutionalize asset maintenance to avoid costly repairs

Barrier: Critical service delivery is disrupted post-disaster

Opportunity: Develop well-coordinated emergency response plans

Source: Vivid Economics.

Maintenance options offer generally favorable returns in promoting resilience. It has been demonstrated that capital costs can increase by 50%–60% (Rozenberg and Fay 2019) because of inadequate maintenance. The World Bank estimates that for every additional $1 spent on road maintenance, $1.50 in investment costs is saved (Kornejew, Rentschler, and Hallegate 2019). For small island developing states, it recommends that improved maintenance of the transport network be priorized to improve resilience. In the power sector, maintaining vegetation along transmission lines can be a cost-effective way of reducing vulnerability to strong winds, and hence the incidence of power outages and high repair costs (Hallegatte, Rentschler, and Rozenberg 2019).

Operational models that effectively prioritize user needs can allow network operators to respond to changing circumstances, thereby enhancing operational resilience. Designing operations in a way that allows operators to adjust to regular changes in supply and demand puts them in a better position to continue to provide an acceptable level of infrastructure services after a disaster occurs. This is known as operational resilience. In the focus group discussions, for example, stakeholders in the water sector of Bangladesh identified increased use of information technology, regular monitoring, and investment in local training as some of the most effective operational mechanisms for improving infrastructure resilience. The built-in flexibility makes critical services more likely to continue to be delivered even with a degraded infrastructure network, especially during high-frequency, low-impact disasters.

Energy networks can incorporate supply- and demand-side mechanisms to balance the network load. When the network is affected by a disaster, these mechanisms can be activated either to increase generation or to manage demand. Figure 19 provides examples of how flexible operational approaches differ by sector and according to the type of service delivered.

Figure 19: Examples of Operational Flexibility to Support Infrastructure Resilience in the Power and Water Sectors

Operational resilience in the power sector

In the power sector, shocks tend to be rapid. Electricity networks are usually highly interconnected within a country, allowing geographically flexible responses but possibly generating cascading risks.

Day-to-day resilience is achieved by maintaining standby capacity, which is sized to absorb shocks up to the threshold of intolerable risk, such as the loss of a single power plant. The interconnected nature of the transmission network also allows operators to rebalance supply and demand across geographic regions. Operators of sophisticated power grids can also manage demand through demand-side response.

During a disaster such as an earthquake, transmission system operators can quickly lose several generators and large portions of the transmission network simultaneously. They can prioritize services for essential infrastructure such as hospitals, railways and airports, while disconnecting non-essential customers. They also maintain rapid response units, which can quickly repair damaged power lines and substations.

Operational resilience in the water sector

In the water sector, shocks are often longer-lived. Water networks also tend to be more regionalized than electricity networks, limiting the ability to mitigate spatially correlated shocks.

Day-to-day resilience is achieved by maintaining water reserves in reservoirs. Utilities can diversify water abstraction across geographically and hydrologically dispersed sources including reservoirs, aquifers, and desalinisation plants. Interconnection of regional networks can improve resilience.

During a disaster such as a drought, water utilities can face supply constraints for many weeks or months. Weather forecasts can inform active water supply management. Demand-side interventions such as hosepipe bans can reduce stress.

Source: Vivid Economics.

Planning for disaster response can be informed by risk assessments (discussed in Section 4) and stress-testing. A stress test can assess the extent to which existing mechanisms for active network management and user support can cope with disasters and determine areas that need to be improved (Hall 2021; Hallegatte, Rentschler, and Rozenberg 2019).

Emergency response plans can ensure that the disruption of critical service delivery is reduced. If services are restored rapidly, cascading impact with long-term consequences can more likely be averted or limited in their extent. Emergency protocols define roles and responsibilities for government, network operators, emergency response teams, and other relevant actors. Early-warning systems can detect hazards before they occur, and thus (i) minimize damage and loss by allowing operators to shut down systems in advance, for instance, by moving trains to a safe location; and (ii) speed up response time. Opportunity 10 takes a closer look at emergency response planning.

The stakeholder survey conducted for this report highlights the following priorities in overcoming key barriers to O&M resilience:

- **Providing funding and incentives for asset and network maintenance.** Almost 40% of survey respondents indicated that dedicated funding is the most needed improvement for O&M resilience. Despite cost efficiency over the lifetime of the infrastructure, funding mechanisms available to low-income countries may favor capital investments and disaster repair needs. For instance, infrastructure maintenance in Kiribati is limited, as donor funding is typically funneled into replacement rather than upkeep. As a consequence, existing parts of the national infrastructure system may be left more vulnerable to future events. Opportunity 9 offers some approaches to ensure that adequate funding is set aside for maintenance.

- **Understanding how O&M functions contribute to infrastructure resilience.** A better understanding of the types of maintenance activities that support resilience, mapped by hazard and infrastructure sector in combination, would allow infrastructure operators to prioritize their actions and make strategic investments. Some survey respondents pointed out that the danger of disasters to operations and the importance of resilience standards in maintenance are not yet fully understood. The World Bank provides a practical guide to engineering options for improving infrastructure asset resilience by sector. A similar overview for O&M could be a useful resource (Hallegatte, Rentschler, and Rozenberg 2019).

6.2   Opportunity 9: Prioritize Asset Maintenance to Avoid Costly Repairs

Infrastructure maintenance can significantly reduce the need for capital-intensive repair and reconstruction over the lifetime of an asset but is often de-prioritized. Some of the main contributing institutional factors are the following:

- **Constrained short-term budgets can** compel infrastructure operators to cut maintenance budgets. User charges are often constrained by affordability. Financing mechanisms, such as debt, equity, or grants, often restrict use for ongoing expenses. Infrastructure operators can thus be induced to prioritize costly repairs or new investments over regular spending.

- **Regulated asset base mechanisms** (systems in which an economic regulator issues licenses to private companies to charge a regulated price for providing infrastructure services to users [BEIS, United Kingdom, 2021]), where returns depend on the size of the asset base, can encourage investment in capital expenditure.

- **Franchising or contractual arrangements** where the infrastructure owner and the infrastructure operator are separate entities can result in perverse incentives for operators. For instance, an operator may lower its costs by reducing maintenance at the expense of asset quality. This is especially relevant toward the end of a franchising arrangement, when the operator will soon have to return the asset to its owner.

This opportunity explores three ways of addressing these biases. Figure 20 shows the experience of survey respondents in applying these tools (on the left-hand side) and their assessment of how far infrastructure resilience has improved as a result (on the right-hand side).

- **Minimum maintenance standards for assets,** across their lifetime, can enforce good management. This could apply to the quality of the infrastructure assets themselves or to the level of service they provide. Assets beyond their designed lifetime can be assessed to determine whether they should be repaired, upgraded, or replaced. Minimum maintenance standards are used by many of the survey respondents, but not across all assets. Close to 80% said the standards were effective in promoting infrastructure resilience.

- **Asset management systems** that keep track of inventories and asset conditions allow operators to verify compliance with maintenance standards and prioritize assets that are in greatest need of maintenance. While more than 90% of respondents were of the view that asset management systems are effective in improving resilience, less than a third reported that these systems were generally in place in their infrastructure sector. Examples of effective asset management systems come from Belize and Dominica. To better manage road networks, staff in those countries' infrastructure sector were trained to use asset management systems. Their long-term maintenance planning and prioritization of maintenance investments improved as a result (World Bank 2017). Enforcing standards via regular monitoring is important in informing regular risk assessments and asset life cycle management. Effective enforcement mechanisms make maintenance costs a central business requirement, rather than an avoidable cost. Enforcement mechanisms are discussed in more detail in Section 8.

- **Ring-fenced budgets for infrastructure maintenance** can be a useful mechanism for ensuring that adequate funding is available. These become more effective when they are tied to minimum standards of service quality and resilience. Ring-fenced maintenance budgets can improve infrastructure resilience, according to the survey results, yet less than a quarter of respondents reported these to be generally in place in their infrastructure sector.

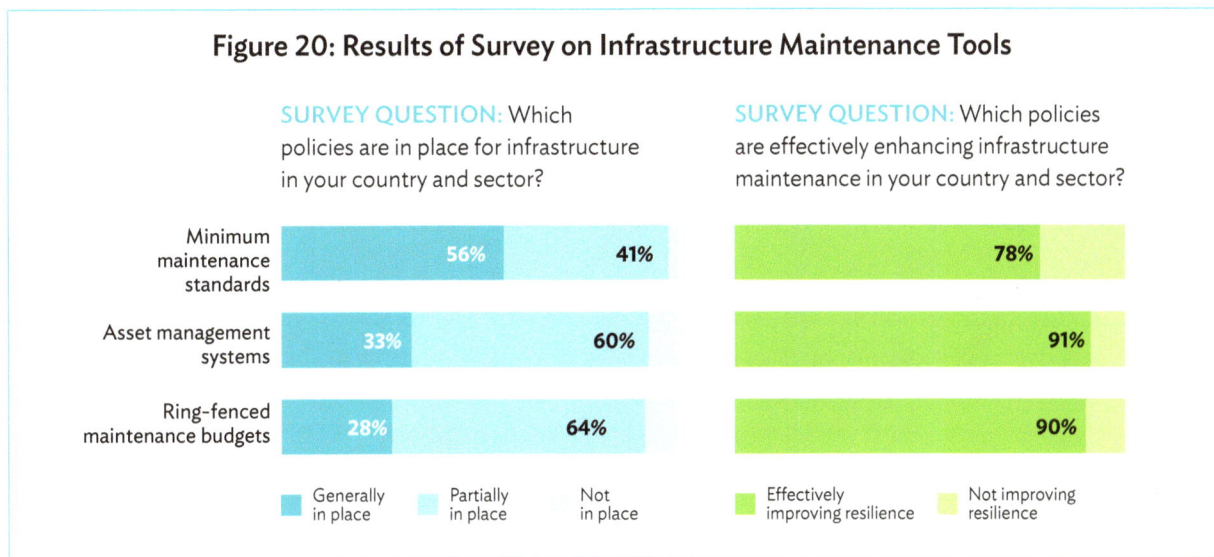

Figure 20: Results of Survey on Infrastructure Maintenance Tools

SURVEY QUESTION: Which policies are in place for infrastructure in your country and sector?

SURVEY QUESTION: Which policies are effectively enhancing infrastructure maintenance in your country and sector?

	Generally in place / Effectively improving resilience	Partially in place	Not in place / Not improving resilience
Minimum maintenance standards	56%	41%	
Asset management systems	33%	60%	
Ring-fenced maintenance budgets	28%	64%	
Minimum maintenance standards	78%		
Asset management systems	91%		
Ring-fenced maintenance budgets	90%		

Source: Vivid Economics, based on data from stakeholder survey.

6.3   Opportunity 10: Develop Well-Coordinated Emergency Response Plans

Essential services depend on several infrastructure networks. Service restoration after a disaster therefore requires coordination among operators. At the same time, infrastructure networks are interdependent: failure in one network can lead to service disruptions in another. Coordination is needed to prioritize the restoration of assets that are required for other networks to function.

It is important to make information and resources available where they are most needed to recover quickly from disasters. Data and information from network-level risk assessments and stress tests must be shared, and the likely effects of impact in one sector on interdependent networks must be assessed. Intolerable risk levels must also be jointly defined, and actions to be taken when these occur must be agreed on. The Government of Bangladesh, for example, has successfully enhanced the country's emergency recovery options by setting up a nationwide optical fiber network. Operators are now better able to establish alternative routes for communication, to support the network in reducing the impact of disasters on users and in restoring full operability in a timely fashion post-hazard.

Public communication during and after disasters is essential. This was demonstrated in New Zealand, after the 2011 Christchurch earthquake. The power distribution company Orion used a live geographic information system (GIS) to enhance public communication. This generated a real-time map showing areas of the city where power was available, and the status of ongoing repairs. It allowed public institutions, health-care facilities, households, and businesses to make informed plans about how and when they could use the services. Governments also increasingly use social media as a platform for interacting with users to coordinate emergency relief.

In some instances, pooled financing mechanisms can provide efficient help in restoring essential services. Mutual aid agreements can facilitate the pooling of resources across an alliance of utilities. They work best in settings of public ownership and clarity in resource costs, where participants agree to provide technical and resource assistance to individual utilities that have gone through a disaster.

Mechanisms for learning from previous disasters in other geographies and sectors can improve emergency response planning. Platforms like SOURCE (SIF, n.d.) (see Box 12 in the next section) bring together practitioners to share data and best-practice examples.

The results of focus group discussions suggest that in Nepal's transport sector, dedicated funding and teams are in place for road maintenance after disasters. If not maintained, local roads are often closed during the whole monsoon season. Dedicated teams maintain roads during the monsoon season, removing debris from landslides. An NRs10 billion emergency response fund allocates 5% to operations and 20% to maintenance.

In Nepal's water sector, O&M is often prioritized in large national infrastructure projects, but less so in smaller or privately led projects. The coincidence of the monsoon season and the financial year-end means that funding for much-needed O&M is often depleted by the time Nepal experiences many of its most extreme flood events.

7   Scaling Up Financing for Infrastructure Resilience and Disaster Response

7.1   Overview

Resilient infrastructure systems require financing to support interventions that will reduce risks and respond to disasters. This section explores financing models across risk reduction and residual risk management, in two main areas (see Figure 21):

- **Resilient infrastructure financing.** Financing for investments in interventions that increase the disaster preparedness of an infrastructure system and reduce risks before a disaster occurs. Such investments in risk reduction are relatively low-cost—a study of power, water, and sanitation in low- and middle-income countries estimates these costs at 3% of overall capital costs (Hallegatte, Rentschler, and Rozenberg 2019)—and can be cheaper than post-disaster repairs, hence unlocking longer-term savings.

- **Disaster risk financing.** Disaster risk financing (DRF) refers to funds disbursed in the aftermath of a disaster, to pay for emergency response, repair, and longer-term reconstruction needs. DRF is needed to enable infrastructure systems to respond and restore services quickly after severe disasters whose impact cannot be entirely averted with investments in resilience made before the disaster occurred. In practice, insufficiently resilient infrastructure will also require additional financing after a disaster. DRF sources can either be arranged and paid in advance of a disaster (ex ante DRF) or sought after a disaster has struck (ex post DRF).

Figure 21: Financing Mechanisms and Opportunities

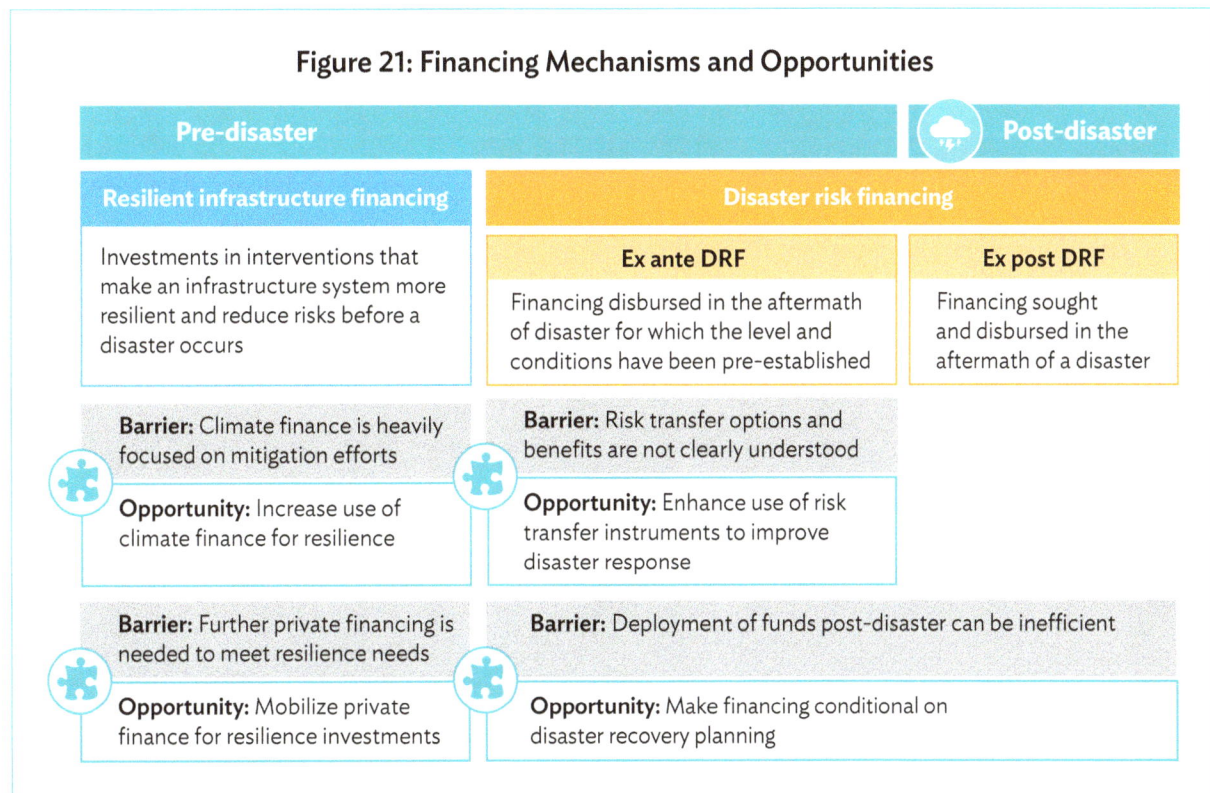

Pre-disaster		Post-disaster
Resilient infrastructure financing	**Disaster risk financing**	
Investments in interventions that make an infrastructure system more resilient and reduce risks before a disaster occurs	**Ex ante DRF** Financing disbursed in the aftermath of disaster for which the level and conditions have been pre-established	**Ex post DRF** Financing sought and disbursed in the aftermath of a disaster
Barrier: Climate finance is heavily focused on mitigation efforts	**Barrier:** Risk transfer options and benefits are not clearly understood	
Opportunity: Increase use of climate finance for resilience	**Opportunity:** Enhance use of risk transfer instruments to improve disaster response	
Barrier: Further private financing is needed to meet resilience needs	**Barrier:** Deployment of funds post-disaster can be inefficient	
Opportunity: Mobilize private finance for resilience investments	**Opportunity:** Make financing conditional on disaster recovery planning	

Source: Vivid Economics.

Financing models must balance investments in infrastructure resilience and disaster response. Higher investment in the resilience of infrastructure before a disaster can reduce response costs, but the investments may limit financial flexibility to cope with cost increases and revenue disruptions after a disaster. Allocating a budget for disaster-proof investments limits the funding available for post-disaster recovery. National budgets can aim for balance between risk reduction investments before disasters and effective disaster response financing to cover the remaining risks. Strategic approaches can integrate risk reduction, preparedness, and response funding into a combined, holistic financial model for optimizing funding across both areas.

There are several types of instruments for infrastructure financing from a range of sources. To finance risk reduction measures, countries and infrastructure providers can use their own resources and revenue streams. Infrastructure projects can also be financed by debt. In many cases, DMCs can have access to grants and concessional loans, subject to eligibility. Concessional loans are loans with favorable terms, such as below-market interest rates, grace periods, extended maturity, and low or no fees. Blended finance and equity investments can also be leveraged. Finally, stakeholders can use transfers, usually in the form of grants and technical assistance, to support resilience projects. ADB provides grants to its 18 poorest DMCs.

The four core financing categories for resilient infrastructure investments are detailed in Table 7.

Table 7: Funding Options for Investments in More Resilient Infrastructure

Category	Instruments	Sources	Benefits	Challenges	
Own resources	• Revenue streams • Reserves	• User fees or taxation	• No conditions attached • No cost of borrowing • Efficient spending incentivized	• Can put pressure on other capital expenditure or operating expenditure, reducing financial resilience • Risk retention • Potential opportunity cost	Back-loaded funding
Debt	• Loans • Concessional loans • Traditional/Green bonds • Development/Environmental impact bonds • PPPs	• Central government • Financial institutions • Development finance institutions • Private investors, potentially FDI	• May incentivize efficient spending (depending on country context)	• Accumulated debt can reduce financial resilience • Debt servicing can put pressure on operating expenditure • Risk retention	Front-loaded financing
Equity	• PPPs • Build–operate–transfer (BOT) schemes • Potentially underpinned by regulatory asset base	• Private investors, potentially FDI	• Additional funding channels (private partners) increase financial resilience • Financial risk reduction (dividends are paid only when owner/operator makes a profit)	• Lack of private investment in sectors with low revenue base • High transaction costs • High losses when PPPs are canceled (~10% of PPPs), including service disruptions and higher risk premiums	
Transfers	• Grants • Allowances for utility owner/operators • Technical assistance	• International aid • Central government • Sector ministries	• Low cost • Risk transfer from infrastructure operator to financing body	• International aid can also be uncertain and unreliable, and carry long lead times until disbursement	

FDI = foreign direct investment, PPP = public–private partnership.
Source: Vivid Economics.

Finance for resilient infrastructure can be complemented by adequate disaster risk financing (DRF) to achieve a holistic resilience financing strategy. It can be categorized as ex ante (arranged before a disaster) or ex post (arranged after the disaster) financing.

Table 8: Funding Options for Disaster Response

Category	Instruments	Most Suitable for	Benefits	Challenges
Ex ante funding	• Insurance schemes • Catastrophe bonds/ Swaps • Contingent financial arrangements • Government contingency budgets and reserves	• Medium-frequency, medium-impact hazards	• Rapid, reliable disbursement • Clearly defined risk ownership • Certainty of available funds encourages better disaster risk management and efficient spending	• Requires continuous financial commitment and planning pre-disaster
Ex post funding	• Budget reallocations • Borrowing • Tax increases • International aid	• Low-frequency, high-impact hazards • Medium-frequency, medium-impact hazards	• Does not require pre-disaster financial commitment or planning from owner/operator	• Uncertainty whether sufficient funding can be secured (timely) in case of hazard • Potential need to pay out of own pocket • May tilt mix of funding away from user fees to tax money
	• Shareholder equity • Owner/Operator's own reserves	• High-frequency, low-impact hazards		

Source: Vivid Economics, adapted from Centre for Global Disaster Protection; Lloyd's (2019).

Ex ante and ex post disaster risk instruments are most effective in combination. Ex ante DRF mechanisms provide important predictability of the magnitude and timing of resources that the government and the infrastructure owners or operators can expect to have available in the aftermath of a disaster. However, as the timing as well as the severity of future disasters is unknown, an excessive reliance on ex ante instruments can leave insufficient flexibility to respond to unforeseen impact. Ex post funds are important mechanisms that allow financing gaps remaining after prearranged (ex ante) funding has been exhausted to be flexibly addressed.

A range of ex ante risk instruments encourage system-wide resilience as well as efficient planning. Traditional indemnity insurance mechanisms provide insurance purchasers with funds for rebuilding specific assets that were damaged during a disaster. They are therefore well-suited to supporting longer-term reconstruction efforts. Alternative structures, such as parametric triggers, can disburse payouts very rapidly (often within days after a disaster strikes), and are therefore particularly suited to supporting shorter-term emergency response and repairs. In addition, risk transfer capacity is available through various channels: for example, catastrophe bonds are tradable high-yield debt instruments that transfer the financial risk of disaster losses to capital markets, which can often offer more attractive pricing than traditional insurance markets.

Ex post financing is aimed at supporting infrastructure operators in maintaining their service provision to users as well as in repairing/reconstructing infrastructure if other funding channels have been exhausted. Ex post disaster response instruments are emergency funds mobilized and disbursed after a disaster occurs and include international and national financial assistance that is mobilized post-disaster, in the form of loans or grants.

Building-back-better principles can guide post-disaster investments to ensure that opportunities to improve resilience to future disasters are seized. Individual assets or entire systems are repaired or reconstructed in a way that improves their resilience compared with pre-disaster levels. These principles imply that response efforts go beyond a "back to normal" functioning and incorporate learning from previous damage to enhance resilience—effectively using post-disaster finance after one disaster to improve pre-disaster preparedness for future disasters.

The majority of infrastructure finance in DMCs is sourced from government or development partners; private finance is particularly limited. Sixty-seven percent of survey respondents indicated that grants from local and national government were their primary source for infrastructure finance, followed by 23% with funding from donors or development banks as their leading source (see Figure 22). Grants from local and national governments can be financed through nationally issued debt. The World Bank Group estimates that a minority—only 1.6%—of overall adaptation financing originates from the private sector.[8] In Bangladesh, stakeholders from the energy sector indicated that there were few incentives in place to encourage private sector investments in infrastructure resilience. Making disaster risk and the benefits of resilience better understood among private finance sources and creating better alignment of incentives between public and private stakeholders are key elements in unlocking additional access to infrastructure finance from private sources. Public–private partnerships (PPPs) can play an important role in reducing existing barriers in these areas (Opportunity 12).

Figure 22: Results of Survey on Sources of Risk Reduction and Preparedness Finance

SURVEY QUESTION:

What is the most important source of funding for disaster preparedness investments in your country and sector?

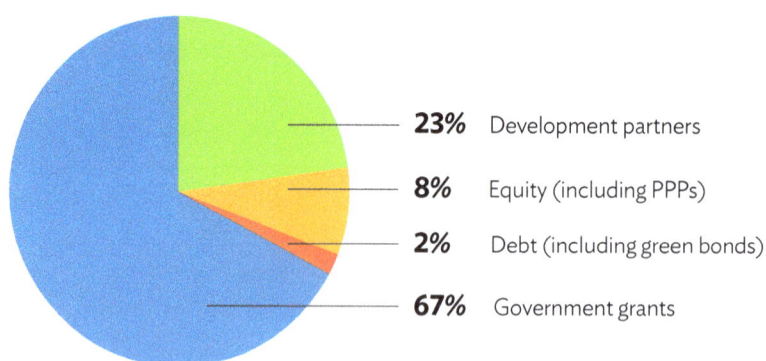

23% Development partners

8% Equity (including PPPs)

2% Debt (including green bonds)

67% Government grants

PPP = public–private partnership.
Note: The response option for "Development partners" originally read, "Donor or MDB grants." This option was interpreted as referring to grants and forms of concessional funding from development partners.
Source: Vivid Economics, based on data from stakeholder survey.

---

[8] A. Tall et al. 2021. *Enabling private investment in climate adaptation & resilience*. Washington DC: World Bank. (Values for 2017-2018)

Use of risk transfer and external contingent mechanisms can be further enhanced in DMCs to finance disaster response. Only 10% of survey respondents indicated insurance to be the primary source of disaster risk financing, while only 17% named contingent financial arrangements as their core financing mechanism (see Figure 23). Given evidence of the efficacy of these approaches (see Clarke and Dercon 2016, for example), there is an opportunity to expand the use of these ex ante mechanisms (Opportunity 13) for DMCs to finance disaster response.

Figure 23: Results of Survey on Sources of Disaster Risk Finance

SURVEY QUESTION:

What is the most important source of funding for disaster preparedness investments in your country and sector?

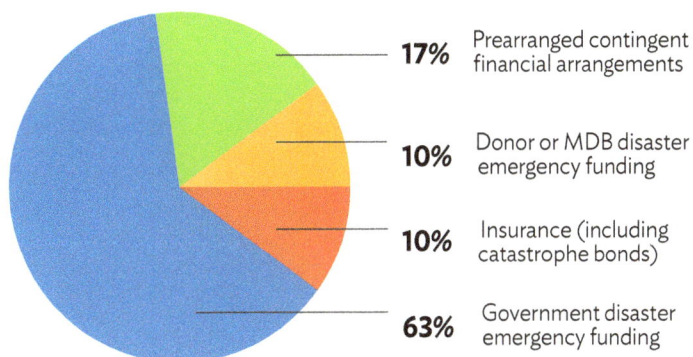

17% Prearranged contingent financial arrangements

10% Donor or MDB disaster emergency funding

10% Insurance (including catastrophe bonds)

63% Government disaster emergency funding

MDB = multilateral development bank.
Source: Vivid Economics, based on data from stakeholder survey.

The stakeholders consulted identified several key barriers to financing resilience. Over 30% of respondents highlighted difficulty in understanding how to balance investment in risk reduction and preparedness with post-disaster recovery and reconstruction as the primary challenge faced (see Figure 24). Expanding the use of instruments linking these two dimensions could deliver further progress toward building resilience (see Opportunity 14). Lack of access to multilateral and donor finance was also deemed a barrier by an equal number of respondents. In survey questions and focus group meetings, stakeholders indicated that donor funding was increasingly difficult to access in the most hazard-exposed areas, because of donor fatigue. Moreover, data and capacity requirements for accessing climate funding options, such as setting up green bond schemes, were deemed too high in certain DMCs. Stakeholders in Fiji highlighted brought out the possibility that the multiplicity of standards for infrastructure resilience set by different donors could make access to these funds even more difficult and constitute an important barrier to accessing financing.

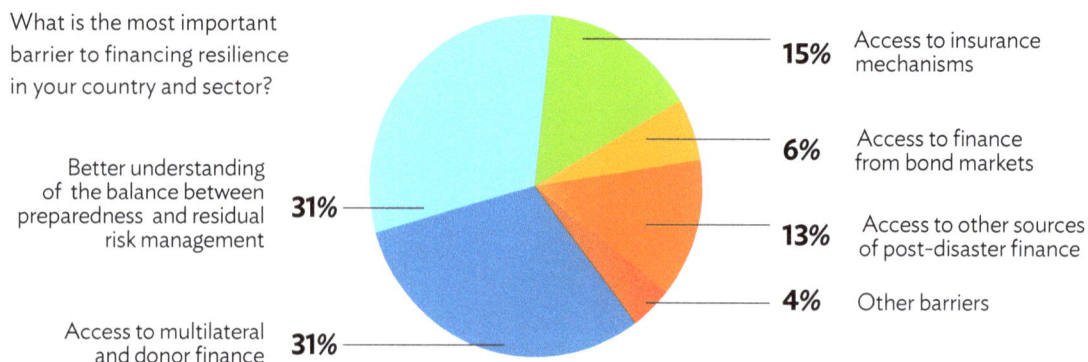

Figure 24: Results of Survey on Barriers to Financing Resilience

SURVEY QUESTION:

What is the most important barrier to financing resilience in your country and sector?

Better understanding of the balance between preparedness and residual risk management — **31%**

Access to multilateral and donor finance — **31%**

15% Access to insurance mechanisms

6% Access to finance from bond markets

13% Access to other sources of post-disaster finance

4% Other barriers

Source: Vivid Economics, based on data from stakeholder survey.

7.2 Opportunity 11: Increase the Use of Climate Finance for Resilience

Climate finance instruments provide funding for investments in resilient infrastructure that may not have been available otherwise. Resilience solutions and related infrastructure upgrades can be a financing challenge for low-income DMCs with budget constraints. Revenue models that can support private sector funding models are potentially important (see Opportunity 12 below) but inherently limited, particularly where user benefits are diffused and often concentrated among low-income groups. Climate finance, including transfers and concessional loans issued by international organizations, governments, or development banks, can play an important role in filling this gap. Climate finance is dedicated to funding climate change mitigation measures and decreasing vulnerability to climate risk. Annual flows of $100 billion in climate finance for developing countries were pledged at the 21 United Nations Climate Change Conference (COP26), and half of this amount is intended for adaptation efforts (UNFCCC, n.d.[a]; COP26 2021).

However, climate finance remains heavily focused on mitigation efforts, and access to affordable funding for resilience-building adaptation is still a challenge. Thirty-one percent of survey respondents mentioned limited access to multilateral finance, including climate finance, as a key barrier to financing resilience in their sector. The limited access can be due to difficulties in meeting current funding requirements, low capacity for project preparation, or lack of funds dedicated to resilience (COP26 2021). While the need for increased adaptation is generally recognized, only around 20%–25% of climate finance is currently targeted at adaptation efforts.[9] Similarly, only 24% of climate finance provided by multilateral development banks (MDBs) in 2020 was spent on adaptation (EBRD et al. 2021). This current imbalance between mitigation and adaptation finance highlights the opportunity to develop better channels for connecting the large pool of available climate finance commitments with specific investments in infrastructure resilience. Lastly, when available, funding for adaptation is often project-focused and encourages asset-level resilience, because of challenges in capturing system-wide risks and benefits, similar to the challenges that hinder resilience investments in general (see Sections 4 and 5).

Governments can leverage existing international platforms for climate finance to systematically identify

---

[9] United Nations Framwork Convention on Climate Change Standing Committee on Finance. 2021. Fourth (2020) Biennilal Assessment and Overview of Climate Finance Flows. Bonn.

available sources for resilience investments. DMC governments can increase the use of existing tools like the United Nations Framework Convention on Climate Change (UNFCCC) Climate Finance Data Portal, which lists and informs potential climate financing sources available, to ensure that new international financing sources are systematically taken into account and effectively leveraged to scale up investments (UNFCCC, n.d.[b]). This will also help DMCs get an overview of current funding requirements.

Better information about system-wide risks and benefits can help to channel more climate finance toward resilience investments in infrastructure. As discussed in preceding sections, the value of infrastructure resilience is often underestimated in current approaches to risk assessment and cost–benefit analyses. Providers of climate finance therefore have an incomplete view of the range and scale of opportunities to invest in adaptation investments. Improving risk information can address this challenge by providing a more holistic view of adaptation opportunities and their benefits, and ensuring that these are matched with available climate finance commitments. In the climate-resilient port in Nauru (Box 11), for example, grand financing has been provided, following an effective evaluation of future disaster risk.

Box 11: Climate Grant Financing for a Climate-Resilient Port in Nauru

Nauru's 11,300 inhabitants receive many of their essential supplies via sea link; however, chronic and acute climate hazards may render their port less reliable. Nauru depends substantially on its seaport for essential supplies—such as food, energy, and other necessities—because of its isolated location in the Pacific. The projected rise in sea level, as well as the increased frequency and severity of cyclones and storms, may, however, make the port inoperable for extended periods throughout the year.

The Asian Development Bank, the Green Climate Fund (GCF), and the Australian government financed the construction of a climate-resilient port for Nauru, which can operate year-round. In 2017, ADB agreed to provide grant financing of $21 million for climate-resilient port infrastructure, cofinanced by the GCF and the Government of Australia. The upgraded port infrastructure is due to be completed in 2023 and will feature a channel for oceangoing ships, a wharf, a berth pocket, and a breakwater to shelter facilities from waves.

To support the long-term efficiency of the investment, additional institutional and operation and maintenance (O&M) measures will be put in place. The Nauru Port Authority will also establish institutional reforms to guide port governance and management. It likewise plans to set up a fund for the sustainable O&M of the new assets, with some initial financial support from the government, to be phased out later.

Source: NMPA (n.d.).

Increased financing for infrastructure resilience also depends on improved information about the incremental cost of building resilient infrastructure. Such information will support DMCs and infrastructure operators in making cost comparisons between resilient designs and alternatives, and subsequently in securing the appropriate level of financing. Indeed, while the cost of integrating disaster resilience into infrastructure projects can vary notably, early and appropriate consideration of options can significantly limit—or, in certain cases, even reverse—this cost and enable DMCs to improve resilience at little or no expense.

Clear and consistent disclosure of adaptation benefits across infrastructure projects can make the value of disaster-resilient infrastructure systems more visible and comparable. As disaster resilience is often not the main driving force behind large infrastructure projects, it may not be automatically considered for adaptation finance. A standardized "resilience certification" process, which systematically reviews projects for adaptation benefits, could help to increase the visibility of infrastructure investments. This, in turn, could provide a clear overview of resilience investments for climate finance providers. The certification could be directly linked to system-wide risk information, as discussed previously.

Sharing best practices related to climate finance outcomes within governments and across the region can help in scaling up the use of climate finance for investments in resilient infrastructure. Institutional networks that share expertise and experiences can help to overcome initial capacity or knowledge gaps. Incentives can thus be created for increasing support for climate finance, and further funding for resilience projects can be more easily obtained. Archetypal models for the scale-up of investments, as well as for a programmatic approach, can be encouraged; these will ensure that the necessary funding is made available. Platforms like SOURCE (see Box 12) could be leveraged systematically by policy makers and project managers to encourage system-wide consideration and build a compelling case for investments in infrastructure resilience from climate finance (and other) sources.

7.3 Opportunity 12: Mobilize Private Financing for Resilience Investments

Private financing can play an important role in supporting infrastructure resilience. The private sector can provide financial capacity that the public sector alone cannot meet (Panwar 2021), besides incentivizing cost efficiency and innovation.

Public–private partnerships (PPPs) are mechanisms through which private financing can support investment in public infrastructure. Typically, the private partner bears the up-front investment, thereby loosening capital constraints, and recoups its investment over time through payments that can be made contingent on performance. Some PPPs repay the private funding according to a regulated asset base model, under which performance standards and terms of payment can be set more flexibly than through a contract, though this requires highly credible institutions that ensure investors receive a fair rate of return.

However, the business case for private investment in resilient infrastructure is perceived as weak and resilience investments from private entities are mostly centered on highly profitable areas. In part, this focus reflects a general tendency for resilience to be undervalued in investment appraisal (see Section 5) or valued only in areas where high benefits can be secured. For example, stakeholder engagement with the telecommunications sector of Bangladesh indicates that if private investors on occasion consider resilience factors in site selection, they take complementary steps to address natural hazards only in highly profitable areas. The focus on profitability also reflects a lack of developed risk-sharing and revenue mechanisms for PPPs, giving investors little incentive to invest in resilience. With climate change, this lack of incentives is likely to be magnified, as resulting future risks are in most cases not clearly allocated in current PPP contracts, leading to investor uncertainty (ADB 2021c).

DMCs and their development partners can deal with these barriers and increase private financing of resilience by developing credible revenue models that efficiently allocate the costs and benefits of investing in resilience. Standardized revenue models, which consider the costs and benefits in all areas of the "triple dividend," can help to establish a clear division of responsibilities and create new incentives for private sector commitment. Such mechanisms can include forward-looking incentives related to asset condition, insurance requirements, or the responsibility of private investors to bear the cost of service outages due to natural hazards if certain resilience standards are not met. Incentives to price disaster risk appropriately and to assign a favorable value to resilient assets can also be put in place. These frameworks can be developed with the support of a broader range of development partners. Revenue-sharing mechanisms should be underpinned by credible institutional arrangements, which give private investors confidence that commitments made to them will be met (see also Section 8). Support from multilateral organizations like MDBs may help to establish such credibility, particularly in the initial phases of an investment.

In addition, DMCs can define models that clarify disaster risk allocation between parties in PPPs. Currently, the majority of PPP contracts do not explicitly clarify roles and responsibilities related to disaster risk and resilience. Even where the assets are privately owned, the public sector is implicitly expected to support the response to major disruptions due to natural hazards (ADB 2021c). Explicit allocation of risk will often require compensation for investors. This approach sets a baseline from which future changes can be negotiated. Incentives from the public side enabling private partners to take on part of the risk without increasing costs drastically can initially support uptake. In the longer term, explicit allocation will increase visibility and understanding of disaster risk and resilience benefits across the private sector. This can, in turn, unlock natural market forces for taking risk and resilience increasingly into account in private investment decisions, through pricing mechanisms, for instance.

Offering a pipeline of projects can also help the private sector to discern a larger long-term value in investing in resilience. Governments can offer a pipeline of public procurement or PPP infrastructure projects that build resilience, such as flood defenses. This project pipeline can help demonstrate an attractive scale of opportunities for private finance. Confidence in the long-term viability of resilient infrastructure as an area for attractive investments can overcome the potential reluctance of private sector stakeholders to invest in the up-front costs of building capacity to engage effectively in this area. These costs may arise from navigating local regulatory and procurement processes or building risk assessment capabilities. A strong, credible pipeline of opportunities can assure investors that such initial costs are worthwhile investments, unlocking an attractive business stream for them. The SOURCE platform (see Box 12) has proven to be an effective mechanism for aligning sustainable PPP pipelines with private sector expectations and international best practices.

Box 12: SOURCE Platform

SOURCE, a multilateral platform for improving the sustainability of infrastructure, provides governments with guidance and templates for all stages of the project life cycle, and thereby supports the development and digitization of resilient infrastructure projects. It was designed to directly address specific targets of the Sustainable Development Goals and the Paris Agreement, and can be connected to national information technology systems to include local considerations.

The platform has a track record of support for PPPs. SOURCE supports infrastructure projects in aligning with international standards and best practices, which have been designed in close cooperation with the private sector. The platform allows stakeholders to coordinate and digitize the project agenda, thereby creating a common understanding between developers, bidders, and investors. The resulting transparency and standardized project management procedures make private investment immediately achievable.

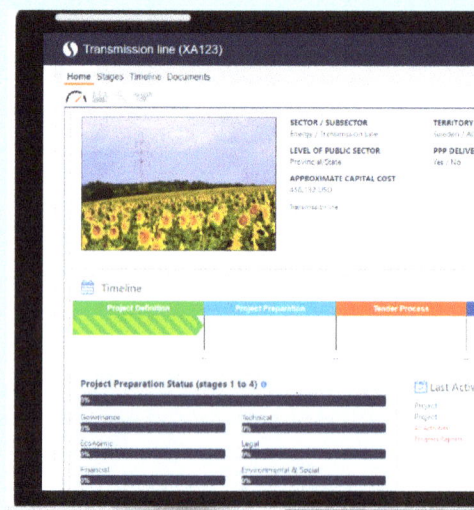

ADB has integrated SOURCE into various PPP portals across Asia and the Pacific. ADB used the platform in developing portals for national PPP centers, for example, in Azerbaijan, Indonesia, Kazakhstan, the Philippines, and Uzbekistan. SOURCE-facilitated assistance is ongoing in these countries. Other countries in Asia and the Pacific, such as India, Mongolia, and Viet Nam, have established early contact with the platform or are preparing for integration.

Building on existing examples, SOURCE could gain wider use and further increase the role of PPPs—and private finance more broadly—in infrastructure resilience. Besides greater use of the platform, an expansion in its content could also be made in the future, to include system-wide resilience considerations and enable PPPs to take a more holistic view of resilience improvements.

ADB = Asian Development Bank, PPP = public–private partnership.
Source: SIF (n.d.).

7.4   Opportunity 13: Enhance the Use of Risk Transfer Instruments to Improve Disaster Response

Transferring risk in advance of disasters provides planning certainty for post-disaster interventions. A lack of prior understanding of how relief and recovery will be funded can slow down the process and make it less efficient, and creates disincentives for "forward-looking" approaches to disaster response. The use of ex ante risk transfer arrangements can therefore reduce both losses from disasters and the costs associated with relief and recovery efforts. However, despite evidence of the cost-effectiveness of ex ante measures, disaster risk financing (DRF) mechanisms often remain focused on ex post disaster relief (ODI 2013).

Survey respondents flagged the shortage of information and incentives as a critical barrier to the uptake of ex ante DRF (see Figure 28). Stakeholder consultations indicated that in Nepal, and particularly in its water sector, insurance is in place for large infrastructure assets like hydropower projects but is typically absent for smaller and rural projects. Similarly, in Viet Nam, survey respondents noted that the provision of insurance services for most infrastructure sectors was insufficient. The survey identified the need for a better understanding of how investments in pre-disaster preparedness can be balanced with post-disaster response, indicating that the low uptake of risk transfer mechanisms may stem from uncertainties around value and use cases. The survey also showed the necessity of providing more in-depth knowledge of the various risk transfer instruments that are available. The benefits of infrastructure risk insurance must be demonstrated further to improve endorsement, according to survey respondents. Uptake by infrastructure operators can be inhibited as well by the perceived availability of post-disaster emergency funding from national and international public sectors.

A clearer understanding of the value, availability, and applicability of risk transfer instruments can promote their uptake among governments and infrastructure providers, and increase the predictability of funding available after a disaster. This section provides an overview of key DRF mechanisms and lays out their applicability to different stakeholders and use cases.

- **Indemnity insurance.** Indemnity products compensate stakeholders for incurred losses from a specified source, up to a pre-agreed limit. The actual level of losses incurred must be demonstrated to the insurance provider for a payout to be made; this process could take several months, or even years. Indemnity insurance is therefore best suited to the transfer of the risk of impact, which can be easily measured in a post-disaster context. For example, damage to physical assets can be objectively assessed, whereas the financial loss associated with emergency response operations is harder to quantify. Moreover, indemnity insurance is typically unsuitable for immediate response and recovery needs, which require access to finance shortly after a disaster, as a long period could pass before a payout is disbursed. For this reason, indemnity insurance is most useful in the context of longer-term reconstruction efforts, often made by the infrastructure providers themselves.

- **Parametric insurance.** Unlike indemnity insurance payouts, the payouts from parametric products do not depend on actual losses incurred but can be triggered by hazards with predefined characteristics like wind speed or flood depth. This trigger mechanism offers two key advantages. First, it can be used as a basis for receiving payouts that are not conditional on specific losses. Second, payouts can be disbursed rapidly in the wake of a disaster, as they do not rely on an assessment of losses. These features make parametric insurance particularly suitable for governments and infrastructure operators in need of funds for relief and early-recovery costs shortly after a disaster.

For both indemnity and parametric insurance mechanisms, the type and scale of coverage chosen can match context-specific priorities and constraints. Insurance is relevant to all DMCs, as the amount of financial commitment can be adapted to context-specific hazard and income levels. While premiums must be paid as an ongoing financial requirement pre-disaster, the amount of such payments is determined by the country's hazard exposure and ability to pay. For example, low-income countries with high hazard levels can reduce the cost of insurance by leveraging insights gained from risk assessments (see Section 4) to identify high-priority areas for their insurance program (e.g., specific types of hazards and/or geographic areas) and focus coverage on these. Basic protection can still be provided against financial losses from disasters, while keeping premium costs low. International insurance markets can support DMCs where the private insurance market is limited or nonexistent in gaining access to insurance products. With the experience acquired in international markets, DMCs can eventually develop robust internal markets and appropriate regulatory frameworks themselves.

- **Catastrophe bonds (cat bonds).** Cat bonds allow governments to transfer risk to capital markets, in much the same way as in traditional insurance schemes. The bond issuer is paid by the capital market investor if a disaster meeting a predefined threshold occurs before the bond maturity date. In return, the investors purchasing the bond receive regular interest payments, analogous to insurance premiums. Cat bonds typically mature 3–5 years after issuance, at which point the purchaser of the bond receives back the investment, less payouts made to the issuer. Cat bonds can be associated with high institutional requirements, as they require planning capacity, financial expertise, and international cooperation, and transaction costs are high. Uptake can thus be limited to select DMCs with high GDP and institutional capacity. Their setup can, however, be supported by multilateral development banks (see Box 13). Cat bonds are typically sovereign bonds. Therefore, they are most suitable for public utilities, often those in the water and transport sectors. The proceeds of sovereign cat bonds can be channeled into private utilities as an emergency funding mechanism.

- **Contingent disaster financing.** Contingent disaster financing instruments are financing lines of credit or grants established pre-disaster that provide immediate liquidity after a disaster occurs. They are triggered by events that meet preestablished criteria, such as the declaration of a state of emergency in a country, in accordance with its legislation, and are therefore generally quick-disbursing instruments. For example, contingent disaster financing from ADB is available to all DMCs and can take the form of credit lines or grants, depending on the classification of the DMC concerned. Contingent disaster financing is predominantly issued in US dollars or euros and is therefore more relevant in the case of governments needing to maintain a stable exchange rate for the local currency.

- **National contingent financing arrangements (NCFAs).** To make these arrangements, governments pool reserves continuously from infrastructure owners/operators before a disaster strikes. The collected resources are used post-disaster to finance reconstruction. NCFAs provide a high degree of national ownership and can be disbursed quickly, and they do not require international support. But the implementing governments must already have in place policies that require infrastructure owners/operators to contribute a certain share of their annual profits to the emergency fund. Such policies are most effective in countries where corruption is low. NCFAs are also more likely to be successful in DMCs where at least some infrastructure sectors are privatized. On the other hand, if the infrastructure sectors are in the public domain, the total financial commitment is effectively borne by the government, making NCFAs a costly option.

Box 13: Sovereign Catastrophe Bond, Philippines, 2019

A sovereign catastrophe (cat) bond in the Philippines was the first government-issued cat bond in Asia. It is supported by the World Bank. In 2019, the bond transferred a total of $225 million in potential financial exposure from earthquakes and tropical cyclones to the international capital markets, for a period of 3 years.

This cat bond provides the Philippines with quick access to funds after a catastrophe, to support relief and early recovery efforts without having to divert financial resources from other areas like infrastructure development.

In December 2021, Typhoon Rai (known as Super Typhoon Odette in the Philippines) triggered a payout of $52.5 million from the cat bond, as part of its tropical cyclone coverage.

Sources: World Bank (2020a); Evans (2022).

7.5 Opportunity 14: Make Finance Conditional on Disaster Recovery Planning

- **Disaster recovery plans are essential in ensuring long-term resilience but do not always exist at subnational levels.** Robust pre-disaster planning for recovery ensures that funding disbursed following a disaster is spent efficiently and can be as impactful as possible. Disaster recovery plans are often established at the national level, and are less common at the sector and infrastructure provider level, according to stakeholder consultations.

- **Linking financing to recovery planning requirements offers an opportunity to improve capacity to respond effectively to disasters.** Existing mechanisms, as well as emerging novel approaches, actively establish this link. The concrete examples they provide can be scaled up across the region to maximize the long-term resilience benefits of post-disaster finance.

- **Existing mechanisms, whose uptake can be increased further, include insurance conditions and contingent funding for infrastructure sector operators.** DMCs can set access criteria for these contingent funding sources, such as obligations to design appropriate disaster risk management plans, conduct risk assessments, consider nature-based solutions, or purchase insurance protection. Requirements can be established alongside capacity-building resources to progressively meet the defined conditions. For example, access to certain emergency and reconstruction funds from Mexico's Natural Disaster Fund (see Box 14) is accompanied with incentives to enhance disaster risk management.

- **Novel approaches continue to emerge and can lead to new and broader use cases.** Innovative mechanisms include insurance-linked loan packages (infrastructure loans with built-in insurance), resilience impact bonds (pay-for-performance contracts), resilience bonds (risk transfer mechanisms similar to cat bonds that explicitly consider resilience measures in premium calculation), and resilience service companies (agents implementing resilience measures to access insurance premium discounts) (see also Table 9). Insurance-backed loan packages, for instance, are concessional loans with resilience conditions, which automatically include disaster insurance coverage for assets financed through the loan (Lloyd's 2019). By explicitly integrating risk transfer solutions in this way and combining the purchase of loan and insurance into a single procurement process, they reduce the administrative burden of finance arrangements and incentivize insurance uptake. Practical examples of these innovative mechanisms currently remain limited, making it important for initial lessons and successes to be shared in order to enable further refinement and increased adoption.

Table 9: Innovative Mechanisms Balancing Infrastructure Financing and Disaster Response

Instrument	Description	Benefits	
Insurance-backed loan packages	These are (concessional) loans with resilience conditions, including insurance of assets. Insurance cost may be included in the loan amount.	The loans explicitly integrates risk transfer solutions into debt instrument, thereby reducing administrative burden of finance arrangements	The instruments involve (at least implicitly) insurance coverage for resilient assets with the dual benefit of: • ex ante response financing • risk transfer
Pay-as-you-save (PAYS) schemes	A resilience services company (ReSCo) is an independent agent that pays for and implements resilience measures in exchange for returns from future insurance premium discounts. An analogous example exists in the energy sector but is untested in insurance.	Retains financial resilience and operational expenses at previous (or slightly improved) levels as *Payment to ReSCo ≤ Non-resilient insurance program*	
Resilience impact bonds	A pay–for–performance contract in which private investors cover the costs of providing various aspects of resilience and are repaid by a donor based on the benefits of the project (measured by insurance rebate).	The bonds provide investors with strong incentives to meet all required resilience measures in a cost-efficient manner	
Resilience bonds	Resilience bonds are risk transfer mechanisms similar to cat bonds that explicitly consider resilience measures in their premium calculation.	The bonds provide strong incentives for investors to put in place projects with large resilience benefits	

Source: Vivid Economics.

Box 14: FONDEN—Funding Allocated with Requirements

Mexico's Fondo de Desastres Naturales (FONDEN) is a fund through which the government makes ex ante budget allocations for the recovery of critical public infrastructure following a disaster. Projects financed include not only the replacement but also the upgrading of damaged assets in order to reduce future damage.

Stakeholders applying for FONDEN resources after a disaster must show proof that their planned reconstruction projects include elements designed to reduce future damage from natural hazards. There are also limits on eligibility for repeat financing for uninsured assets, intended to encourage project managers to purchase insurance.

Source: World Bank (2012).

8 Designing Institutions to Support Infrastructure Resilience

8.1 Overview

Institutional arrangements can promote resilience by setting credible long-term incentives, promoting cross-sectoral coordination, and developing capacity. This section explores the role of institutions in achieving resilience objectives through a variety of regulatory, financial, coordination, and capacity levers, and presents opportunities for using those levers to meet the objectives.

Resilient infrastructure investments and effective disaster response typically benefit society greatly, making resilience improvements and planning worthwhile investments. While the investments needed to make infrastructure more resilient are substantial, benefits, in the form of avoided loss of life, sustained economic activity, and avoided or reduced damage, typically outweigh these costs greatly. For example, ADB (2011) found that road improvements to enhance resilience against flooding, heavy rains, and coastal erosion in Solomon Islands and Timor-Leste resulted in benefit–cost ratios (BCRs) in the 2.16–2.94 range, implying that benefits are more than twice as high as costs. Similarly, coordinating a disaster response plan among relevant stakeholders pre-disaster carries a substantial net benefit; for instance, the Boston Consulting Group (UNICEF and WFP 2015) found that pre-positioning of emergency supplies and staff training yielded savings in terms of cost and time in Chad, Madagascar, and Pakistan.

Institutions must set credible incentives for operators to make resilient long-term investment choices, thereby maximizing benefits to society. Benefits of resilience measures to operators are unknown on account of the uncertain nature of natural hazard occurrences during the asset life cycle. On the other hand, costs are disbursed up-front and recovered over the long term. Therefore, infrastructure operators must have well-aligned incentives that they believe will be honored through effective monitoring and enforcement mechanisms in the present and future. There is also a need for cross-sectoral coordination in defining and enforcing incentives to ensure that these efficiently deliver targeted resilience benefits to infrastructure users. The capacity and stability of institutions determine how well and credibly such incentives are designed, and therefore how effectively they succeed in fostering long-term planning and resilience benefits.

Incentives can include regulatory, financial, and structural levers, which may be used individually or in combination to effectively achieve different priorities:

- **First, governments and local authorities can strengthen infrastructure resilience through regulatory levers and effective enforcement mechanisms for monitoring compliance.** Regulatory mechanisms are "command and control" measures that are set and enforced centrally. A variety of regulatory mechanisms for setting minimum resilience standards are available to governments; these include building codes, spatial planning or zoning frameworks, and risk-informed urbanization. Moreover, governments can alter operators' degree of independence to promote long-term resilient decision-making. In order to be credible, each regulatory lever must have a supporting structure for effective enforcement and compliance monitoring. There are different approaches to enforcement, including third-party institutions, independent surveyor reports, evidence requirements, and peer "checks and balances."

- **Second, monetary incentives and disincentives are useful mechanisms for encouraging voluntary uptake of comprehensive resilience measures.** Financial penalties and rewards are tools designed to incentivize operators to go beyond the minimum standards set in regulations. Monetary levers include taxes and subsidies, financial mechanisms for disaster risk reduction, result-based payments, and payments for ecosystem service (PES) schemes. Financial incentives can also be set through regulated tariff structures and changes in the degree of contestability.

- **Third, adjustments can be made in contestability and in the decision-making capacity of operators within an infrastructure sector, through structural changes, to strengthen the focus on resilience.** Contestability refers to "the ease with which new firms can enter and leave the market" (Economics Online 2020). By implication, a higher degree of contestability makes markets more competitive. Increased competition supports innovation and thereby lowers the cost of making infrastructure more resilient, while simultaneously pricing in risk by passing on some of the additional expenses to users ("market-led adaptation"). Standards must also be clearly defined or enforced; otherwise, competitive pressures may lead to underinvestment instead. Central governments must be part of the decision-making process, for resilience efforts to have system-wide application and impact. At the same time, incentives for resilience cannot be effective if local infrastructure operators do not have their own resilience planning and investment responsibilities. Tailoring the degrees of contestability and the sharing of responsibilities between the central government and local stakeholders carefully to the specific context is important in ensuring that the market structure actively fosters resilience and does not lead to unintended adverse incentives.

Stakeholder coordination, both within and across infrastructure sectors, has a significant role in setting incentives that encourage system-wide resilience. Infrastructure operators, sector ministries, the government, and financiers must work together to make sure that resilience efforts are not confined to the asset level but extend to networks and users. Information can be shared, joint objectives set, and standards and incentives aligned across sectors. Governments could also establish a designated disaster risk institution to develop a multi-sector, integrated response management plan.

Centralized capacity building and broader support activities are crosscutting tools that can promote resilience-focused institutions at all levels. Investment in institutional capacity and transparency is useful to a variety of stakeholders while at the same time being relatively inexpensive and having the potential to attract investment. An example of institutional capacity building is technical assistance to operators in analyzing the long-term costs and benefits of resilience measures. Other support activities include the government-led provision of comprehensive disaster risk assessments across all infrastructure sectors.

Survey results suggest that regulatory levers are more commonly in place and enforced than financial levers, but both types are far from reaching full sector coverage. Forty-two percent of all respondents said that regulatory levers were generally in place across their sector, but only 24% said that their sector had existent financial levers (see Figure 25). Evidently, many infrastructure sectors across Asia and the Pacific still lack general coverage of resilience incentives. Respondents also noted that enforcement mechanisms do not fully cover those sectors with regulations and tax incentives in place: less than two-thirds of these regulations and tax incentives were being generally enforced in practice. The gap is especially pronounced for building codes and tax benefits.

Figure 25: Current State of Institutional Levers Supporting Infrastructure Resilience

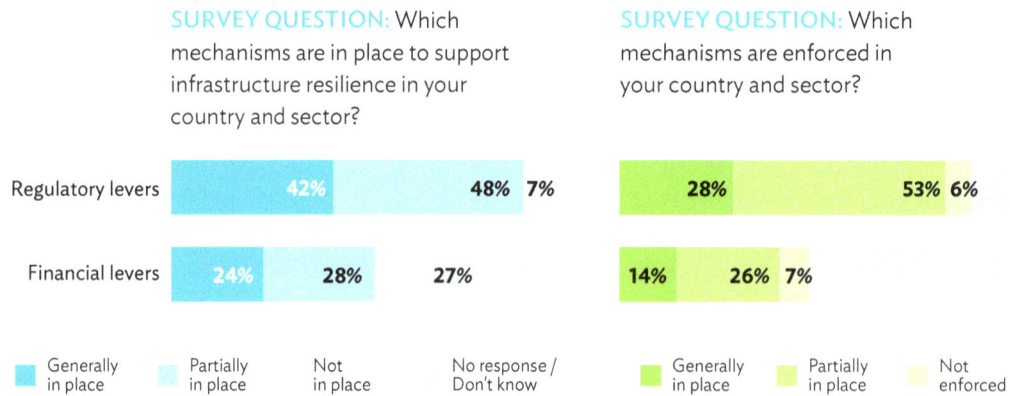

SURVEY QUESTION: Which mechanisms are in place to support infrastructure resilience in your country and sector?

SURVEY QUESTION: Which mechanisms are enforced in your country and sector?

Regulatory levers
42% | 48% 7%
28% | 53% 6%

Financial levers
24% | 28% | 27%
14% | 26% 7%

Generally in place | Partially in place | Not in place | No response / Don't know

Generally in place | Partially in place | Not enforced

Source: Vivid Economics, based on data from stakeholder survey.

The potential for future improvement lies predominantly with enforcement mechanisms, competitiveness structures, and coordination, all of which could help overcome key barriers to resilience. The majority of respondents (43%) identified improved design of regulation based on risk assessments as the most important improvement needed to enhance institutional support for resilience. This includes effective enforcement to create credible incentives—still a key difficulty for DMC governments, according to open-ended survey responses. Additionally, 86% of respondents believe that higher sector competitiveness would strengthen resilience. Focus interviews further identified the political economy of decision-making as a major challenge in advancing resilience in Asia and the Pacific. This is also supported by the open survey responses, which indicate that a key barrier to resilience is the lack of an integrated approach among relevant agencies, both within and across sectors, including insufficient data and knowledge sharing.

Figure 26 provides a high-level overview of the levers available to governments to design institutions that support resilience, including key opportunities. Regulation and enforcement, as well as financial (dis) incentives, are discussed in more detail in Opportunity 15 , while steps to enhance coordination form part of Opportunity 16.

Figure 26: Practical Guide to Designing Institutions to Support Infrastructure Resilience Frameworks

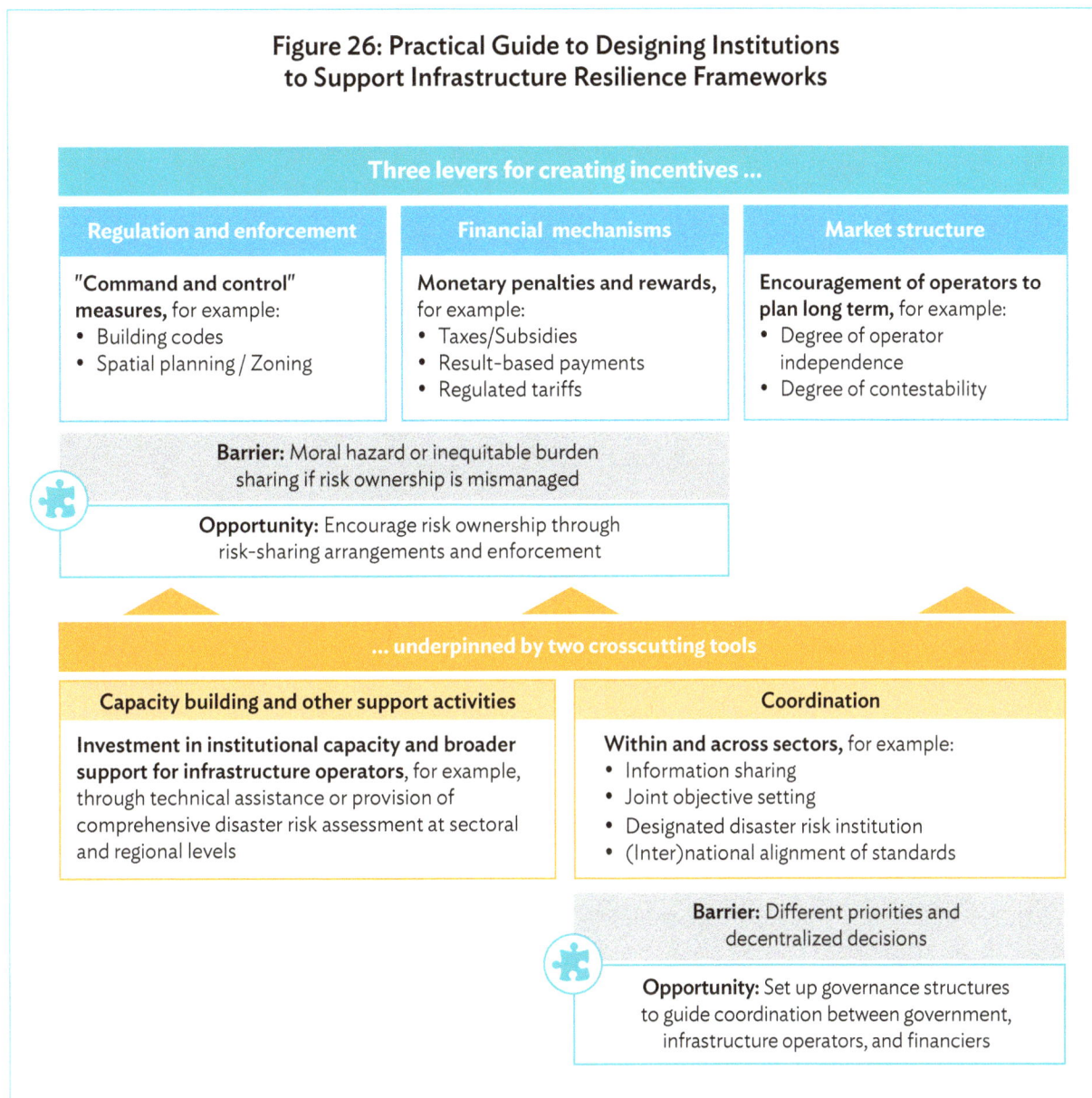

Three levers for creating incentives ...

Regulation and enforcement	Financial mechanisms	Market structure
"Command and control" measures, for example: • Building codes • Spatial planning / Zoning	**Monetary penalties and rewards,** for example: • Taxes/Subsidies • Result-based payments • Regulated tariffs	**Encouragement of operators to plan long term,** for example: • Degree of operator independence • Degree of contestability

Barrier: Moral hazard or inequitable burden sharing if risk ownership is mismanaged

Opportunity: Encourage risk ownership through risk-sharing arrangements and enforcement

... underpinned by two crosscutting tools

Capacity building and other support activities	Coordination
Investment in institutional capacity and broader support for infrastructure operators, for example, through technical assistance or provision of comprehensive disaster risk assessment at sectoral and regional levels	**Within and across sectors,** for example: • Information sharing • Joint objective setting • Designated disaster risk institution • (Inter)national alignment of standards

Barrier: Different priorities and decentralized decisions

Opportunity: Set up governance structures to guide coordination between government, infrastructure operators, and financiers

Source: Vivid Economics.

Country-specific barriers that could hinder the implementation of the highlighted opportunities may exist; this report recognizes that possibility. While the figure above provides an overview of best practices, their effectiveness depends at least partly on the strength of institutions in the country in question. In these cases, the outlined opportunities may not be able to remove all the existing barriers identified. Instead, they can offer a stepping-stone to the eventual removal of the barriers as institutions in the country continue to evolve and strengthen over time.

8.2   Opportunity 15: Encourage Risk Ownership through Risk-Sharing Arrangements and Enforcement

Clarity of risk ownership is required to incentivize risk management. Risk ownership refers to the state in which one clearly defined party is "ultimately accountable for ensuring the risk is managed appropriately" (Office of the Chief Risk Officer, Stanford University, n.d.) If it is unclear whether central governments or infrastructure operators are responsible for the management of risks, neither party will be incentivized to invest in risk mitigation and resilience. The determination of risk ownership is thus an essential first step in setting incentives for resilience.

Risk sharing between governments and infrastructure owners can balance moral hazard and financing costs. If governments commit to bailing out infrastructure operators for chronic or small, frequent hazards, a moral hazard issue is generated, as operators are disincentivized to invest in resilience. On the other hand, owning the risks of infrequent and severe hazards would impose a disproportionate burden on infrastructure operators. Therefore, it is critical for decision makers to find the right balance and put in place appropriate disaster risk finance instruments. Table 10 describes these trade-offs in more detail.

Disaster risk finance mechanisms can be useful in supporting risk ownership by operators. Coordination between risk-sharing arrangements and government-led financing tools is important to ensure they complement each other. Ex ante disaster risk finance mechanisms like insurance or catastrophe bonds spread the costs of operators owning more extreme risks over time, and consequently decrease moral hazard.
Risk ownership relies on credible enforcement. Regulatory and financial levers to incentivize risk management may be difficult and expensive to enforce, and may result in struggles with low compliance among many countries in Asia and the Pacific. However, without credible tools for monitoring and enforce compliance, risk-sharing mechanisms may be ineffective, as infrastructure providers may resort to relying on the government for financial support in case of a disaster (moral hazard issue).

Table 10: Risk-Sharing Mechanisms for Effective Incentive Structures

	Disaster risk borne by operators/owners	Disaster risk borne by government
Benefits	**Resilience investment incentive:** If owners/operators bear the risk of financial losses, they are incentivized to invest in infrastructure resilience improvements. **Response mechanism incentive:** If owners/operators bear the risk of financial losses, they are incentivized to purchase insurance schemes or cat bonds.	**Effectiveness:** Central allocation of funds post-disaster can coordinate response across the infrastructure system. This helps to restore service provision swiftly. **Access to finance:** Governments can access finance at larger scale and through channels unavailable to owner/operators. These mechanisms are often cheaper (emergency relief, contingent disaster financing, grants).
Costs	**User resilience issue:** Lack of timely access to large funds post-disaster can delay response, thereby creating service disruptions and damaging user resilience.	**Moral hazard issue:** Government participation in risk sharing creates disincentive for owners/operators to invest in resilience improvements.
Resolution	The government should establish an **incentive structure** for effective risk sharing with owner/operators. Owners/Operators should bear the risk — Risk should be shared between governments and owners/operators — Governments should bear the risk → Intensity of hazards. *Chronic hazards and small, frequent events* — *Major, rare events*. Owners/Operators should be **obliged** to invest in preparedness for events for which they bear the risk, and **financially encouraged** when the government bears the risk.	

Source: Vivid Economics.

Regulatory levers can be employed by governments to set minimum expected risk ownership by operators. Incorporating resilient infrastructure investments into national and international law ensures that owners and operators take responsibility for the consequences of a certain level of infrastructure exposure to hazards, including chronic hazards. Therefore, regulatory levers establish minimum standards for acceptable performance of infrastructure assets and systems. Operators are typically expected to bear the risk of small, frequent hazards. The following is a practical guide to setting regulatory levers.

- **Building codes** set the standards for disaster-resilient construction. They typically define minimum infrastructure thresholds for resilience against various types of hazards, including storms, earthquakes, and rising sea levels. Reviewing these with respect to future risks is a suitable starting point for regulatory reform.

- **Urban planning and zoning** based on risk assessments reduces the exposure of assets and people by defining and designing targeted regulation for vulnerable areas.

Regulatory levers are well established in some DMCs, but enforcement can be problematic because of capacity constraints. According to stakeholder interviews, both Bangladesh and Indonesia have several of these regulatory mechanisms in place, for example, building codes, certifications, guidelines to ensure the quality of electricity generators and appropriate maintenance, and spatial risk zone planning. However, enforcement depends on the capacity of the responsible authority (central, state, provincial, or local government tiers).

Financial levers can encourage operators to invest in resilience beyond minimum requirements, thereby sharing the risk of more severe hazards with the government. Financial rewards and penalties can create an incentive structure for disaster preparedness. Financial incentives are also useful risk-sharing tools, as they reduce the financial losses covered by the government in case of higher-impact hazards than those the operator is reasonably expected to bear. The types of financial levers are as follows:

- **Tax incentives** are the most common type of financial lever. Financial rewards for resilience compliance, in the form of tax exemptions, tax credits, and subsidies, are typically granted at the time the resilience improvement is made. Tax increases, on the other hand, penalize noncompliance.

- **Result-based payments** are financial rewards that are disbursed only after certain resilience conditions are met. Unlike tax incentives, result-based payments require the owner/operator to incur the full up-front cost of resilience improvements before receiving compensation. A practical example is described in Box 15.

- **Payments for ecosystem services** are schemes through which providers of environmental services, such as natural flood defenses, are rewarded financially. Payments are made by the beneficiaries of the services, for example, the local community that received protection as a result.

Box 15: Result-Based Payments for Housing, Viet Nam

In Viet Nam, a special housing loan and small grant are made available to homeowners that have their homes strengthened against typhoons according to a set of resilience rules. This program is supported by Development Workshop France (DWF).

In order to receive financial support under this program, homeowners must consult with DFW regarding a survey of their homes, the specific work to be done on the structures, and the corresponding financial aid that the homeowners will receive under the program. This result-based payment is accompanied by an awareness-raising program (cultural events, radio and TV broadcasts, etc.) on the importance of typhoon resiliency.

This financial lever has encouraged hundreds of homeowners to strengthen their homes against typhoon damage. The "excellent performance" of hundreds of strengthened buildings during Typhoon Xangsane (2006) and Typhoon Ketsana (2009) confirms the success of the program.

Source: Development Workshop France (n.d.)

Different practical options for effective enforcement can be deployed to support regulatory levers and financial disincentives. Enforcement frameworks are institutions that monitor infrastructure owner/operator performance and penalize noncompliance with resilience standards. Compliance with the standards can be enforced either by the government agencies or by independent third-party institutions. Enforcement through third-party institutions has succeeded in increasing compliance.

8.3 Opportunity 16: Set Up Governance Structures to Guide Coordination Between Government, Infrastructure Operators, and Financiers

Geographic and economic interlinkages between infrastructure sectors within a country mean that hazard impact multiplies if governance is insufficiently integrated. Infrastructure networks are interdependent across sectors and geographies. Therefore, without coordination mechanisms in place to contain the chain of second- and third-order effects, risks can cascade across the system and have catastrophic impact on critical infrastructure service delivery.

Establishing resilience coordination within and between sectors is challenging because of the decentralized nature of decision-making and the differing sets of stakeholder priorities. The actors involved in infrastructure service delivery and financing make up a diverse group with different sets of objectives, their own language, and a unique understanding of infrastructure resilience priorities. For instance, stakeholder interviews found inconsistencies in information sharing between the Nepalese institutions responsible for providing road infrastructure—the Department of Roads, the Department of Provincial Government, and municipalities. Data collection is difficult on account of the large number of municipalities; as a result, the total length of roads in Nepal is unknown. This challenge is even more pronounced for multi-sector coordination and disaster response planning because a larger number of stakeholders are involved, decision-making is more dispersed, and priorities are less aligned.

To establish a sector-wide resilience action plan, stakeholders must share information and invest in a joint understanding of risk and response options. Joint efforts to assess risk, define levels of acceptable risk for individual infrastructure providers, and eventually set sector-wide resilience objectives benefit infrastructure operators, relevant government ministries, and financiers by reducing uncertainties and leveraging interdependencies. Capacity enhancement is a useful mechanism for increasing knowledge exchange about natural hazards and the associated risk for all parties involved. A practical example is described in Box 16.

Box 16: Technical Assistance for Building Code Compliance in Nepal

The city of Dharan in Nepal decided to facilitate compliance with building codes by providing five rules that should be followed in all new construction. As Nepal did not have building codes before 2003, this straightforward set of rules helped to develop human capacity within the building community. The rules were explained to all stakeholders involved and successfully fostered stakeholder cooperation in building development, thus improving the resilience of buildings. This streamlined approach also promoted resilience cooperation with the building community and the government, as the centralized rules ensured that both groups were committed to the same objectives.

Source: UN ESCAP and AIT (2012).

Multi-sector disaster risk institutions bring stakeholders together to develop integrated response mechanisms and governance structures. Measures can be designed to support infrastructure resilience by getting stakeholders together to determine critical infrastructure links and draw up common disaster response management plans. These groupings can be formalized through designated disaster risk institutions. A practical example of dedicated disaster risk institutions can be found in Indonesia, where stakeholder interviews revealed that each hazard is monitored by an established agency depending on the nature of the hazard (meteorology, climatology, hydrometeorology, and geology). These institutions take lead roles in measuring, countering, and recovering from hazards. Responsibilities are also clearly defined for disaster management; for infrastructure, these coordination tasks lie mainly with the sector ministries. Additionally, (inter)national alignment of standards can facilitate implementation and encourage coordination for risk sharing. If standards regarding common risks are aligned, the costs of developing regulations can be reduced for each organization or country.

9 Conclusion and Next Steps

Sustainable development across Asia and the Pacific relies on the resilience of infrastructure systems to the high and increasing disaster risk in the region. The Asia and Pacific region is exposed to disaster risk from a range of natural hazards, whose impact is set to increase amid climate change and urbanization. The resilience of infrastructure to these disasters plays an important part in sustaining and fostering further economic development and social prosperity across the region. Lost opportunities to design infrastructure resiliently, on the other hand, can lock in vulnerabilities for decades to come.

Solutions are emerging to help decision makers understand disaster risk better and prioritize investments that foster system-wide resilience. Disaster resilience of infrastructure is a system-wide characteristic, which cannot be achieved by targeting asset-level resilience standards in isolation. Understanding and managing disaster risks across an entire system can be complex; however, practical, scalable solutions are being developed and can open up important opportunities to promote resilience in Asia and the Pacific.

While conditions differ by location, many challenges are similar and there is significant potential for peer learning and the formation of communities of best practice. Common challenges include a lack of capacity and data for assessing disaster risk, an incomplete view of resilience benefits in cost–benefit analyses underlying investment decisions, and insufficient alignment and coordination of stakeholders. Sharing examples of success and developing a joint understanding of best practices can effectively accelerate improvements in infrastructure resilience and scale these up across the region.

This report contributes toward a joint understanding of key issues and highlights practical opportunities to address those issues. It provides clear guidance on key areas relevant to infrastructure resilience, linking current challenges with opportunities to unlock progress and concrete examples of best practice from the region.

Key opportunities and next steps in achieving improved infrastructure resilience to disasters in Asia and the Pacific include the following:

- gaining a better understanding of the system-wide impact of infrastructure risks and resilience;
- increasing consideration of the "triple dividend" of resilient infrastructure in planning and investment decisions, reflecting not only avoided losses after a disaster but also economic and development co-benefits in the absence of disasters;
- improving coordination mechanisms and alignment of incentives among the various actors involved; and
- providing peer support to promote capacity development and joint learning.

Appendix: Dynamic Adaptive Policy Pathways for Road Resilience to Floods in Cambodia

Introduction

Planning investments in infrastructure resilience can be a challenge because of uncertainty around future risks. Infrastructure assets are durable, long-lived, and often economically important investments. While building infrastructure resilience can be high-cost, maladapted infrastructure can be even more costly to economies and societies. Determining the appropriate level of investment in resilience is complicated by uncertainties surrounding future climate risk, socioeconomic outcomes, and policy options.

The dynamic adaptive policy pathways (DAPP) approach can help decision makers address these challenges by adapting course to meet changing circumstances. Dynamic adaptive policy pathways are a set of sequenced investment actions. These pathways typically involve committing to lower-cost and smaller investment actions in the short term, while also building a framework of potential future actions (Haasnoot et al. 2013). This makes the approach flexible to uncertainty around future conditions and new information.

DAPP highlight insufficiency in resilience levels and the need for further action. They set up a continuous monitoring plan based on trigger and tipping points, where uncertainties and actions must be reassessed (Table A.1) (Haasnoot et al. 2013). Trigger points are external changes indicating that actions need to be taken, like an early warning system. For example, an increase in annual storm events signals a significant change in future weather patterns, which affects flood risks. Tipping points specify the condition under which the status quo will fail. This happens when the magnitude of external change is large enough that a policy can no longer can meet its objectives and further action is required (Haasnoot et al. 2013). For example, an increase in river levels can cause a dike to fail.

Table A.1: Four Main Types of Actions Specified in Dynamic Adaptive Policy Pathways

Type of action	Description	Example
Defensive	Responses to preserve the benefits of the basic plan, leaving the plan unchanged	Reinforce existing infrastructure and maintain resilience objectives
Corrective	Adjustments to the basic plan based on changing risks or new information	Change type of resilience investments specified in basic plan to ensure that the basic plan can continue to support objectives
Capitalizing	Adjustments to the basic plan to take advantage of new, unforeseen opportunities	Begin infrastructure investment earlier than originally planned to take advantage of market for infrastructure
Reassessment	Response required when the assumptions and analysis of the basic plan are evidently no longer valid	Reassess the plan when the trajectory is significantly different from the original forecast

DAPP= dynamic adaptive policy pathway.
Source: Vivid Economics, based on Kwakkel, Walker, and Marchau (2010).

This case study assesses the potential for the DAPP approach to inform flood risk investments in key road segments in Cambodia.[1] It explores different embankment options for making roads more resilient to flooding, in order to demonstrate the potential benefits of early resilience action. While the example is focused on the raising of embankments, as one possible option for managing flood risks to roads, a variety of other resilience-building measures (e.g., smart monitoring, enhanced surface treatments, nature-based solutions) can be used to mitigate flood risk. These are beyond the scope of the study but can form part of a holistic approach to flood risk management with or without dynamic adaptive pathways.

The analysis finds that given the limited uncertainty across climate futures in Cambodia, a strong case can be made for cost-effective and early investments in a high level of protection. While the adaptive pathways approach is typically most informative when uncertainty surrounding climate and socioeconomic futures is high, the case study illustrates that it can still be useful for decision makers even when this is not the case. The approach supports decision makers in building a knowledge base of key risks to infrastructure, determining the implications of investment approaches, and assessing trade-offs between social and economic outcomes.

The rest of the case study is structured as follows:

- First, background information about flood risk to road infrastructure in Cambodia is provided, highlighting how uncertainty analysis could improve the decision-making process.

- Then, step-by-step guidance in developing DAPP is laid out, with reference to examples from the analysis of road infrastructure in Cambodia.

- Finally, the DAPP outcomes and the implications for decision makers are analyzed.

Background: Road Vulnerability to Flooding in Cambodia

Flooding in Cambodia affects 90,000 people and causes $100–$170 million in damage each year (UNDRR Regional Office for Asia and the Pacific and ADPC 2019; World Bank Group and ADB 2021). Cambodia is particularly flood-prone because of its geography: 80% of the country lies within the Mekong River and Tonle Sap basins (Espinet Alegre et al. 2020). The Mekong River basin goes through a flood season from July to November, with 1,200–1,600 millimeters of precipitation yearly (Douven, Goichot, and Verheij 2009). Severe flood seasons can displace local residents. In 2018, for example, the breaching of a dam in the Lao People's Democratic Republic due to extreme weather led to the displacement of more than 6,000 Cambodians (UNDRR Regional Office for Asia and the Pacific and ADPC 2019).

Climate change is increasing weather variability and uncertainty in Cambodia, including the potential for more severe and frequent flood events. Traditionally, flooding brings necessary nutrients for crop cultivation. However, climate change is expected to increase uncertainty around flood frequency and severity (Wight 2014). Some estimates indicate that a flood event that historically occurred once every 100 years could become as common as a 1-in-5-year or 1-in-25-year event (Paltan et al. 2018). More extreme climate change scenarios would lead to more drought conditions in Cambodia that would reduce rainfall, as shown in Figure A.1 below.

---

[1]   Three road segments connecting the northern and southern portions of the country were selected, and thus play a key role in the circulation of goods and people.

Figure A.1: Moderate Warming Increases the Risk of Flooding, but Extreme Warming Has the Reverse Effect

Expected annual damage from flooding over time

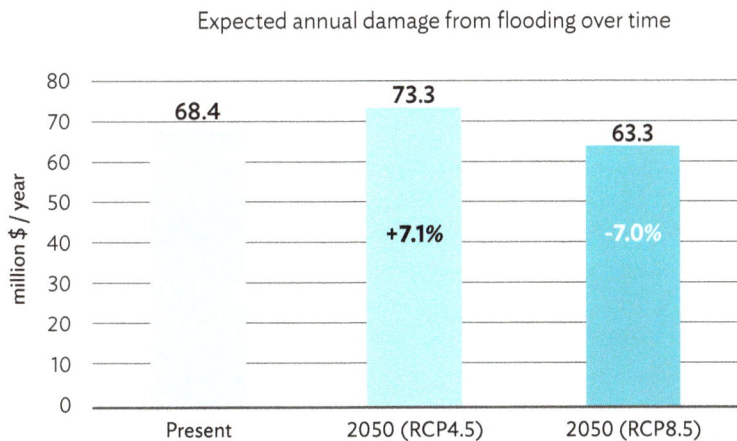

Source: Vivid Economics, for ADB (2021).

Flooding in Cambodia poses risks to road networks, with potential negative consequences for connectivity, livelihoods, and economic development. Cambodia has 20,000 kilometers (km) of national and provincial roads, and 40,000 km of rural roads. Together, these road networks connect Cambodians to markets, health care, and education (MOE, Cambodia, 2017). Around 70% of Cambodians are farmers, and 73% of Cambodian farms engage in subsistence farming (UNDP in Cambodia, n.d.; UNDP 2016). As a result, flooding can limit economic growth potential, particularly in the rural areas:

- **Livelihoods.** Because of the importance of farming, 79% of Cambodians live in the rural areas, making the economy and rural livelihoods particularly vulnerable to damage from road flooding (Leng Heng An 2014; Espinet Alegre et al. 2020). In Kampong Cham, Kratie, and Tboung Khmum provinces, 21% of the total value of agricultural production in the area loses access to markets during floods (Espinet Alegre et al. 2020).

- **Access to critical services.** During severe flooding, the World Bank estimates that 27% of rural Cambodians lose all access to emergency health-care facilities, and an additional 18% have to travel at least 30 minutes more to reach the facilities (Espinet Alegre 2020).

- **Education.** Dropout rates from Cambodian schools are significantly higher during flooding periods than during the dry season. The difference could be due, at least in part, to the challenges of attending school when roads are made inaccessible by flooding (UNDRR Regional Office for Asia and the Pacific and ADPC 2019).

- **Trade.** Road infrastructure provides access to the wider Mekong region. Travel restrictions due to flooding could therefore have implications for trade flow.

Many road networks in Cambodia are currently unable to withstand increased flood risk. Many roads in Cambodia are unpaved and extremely susceptible to washouts during flooding. As of 2017, all national one-digit roads were paved, but only 72% of national two-digit roads, 30% of provincial roads, and 5% of rural roads were paved, making the rest vulnerable to flooding (ADB 2019b).[2] Significant damage and repair costs can result. Recent flooding damaged more than 500 km of national/provincial/urban roads; 200 km of these roads were completely destroyed (NCDM, Cambodia, n.d.). These vulnerabilities particularly affect rural Cambodians: extreme flash flooding in 2020 required more than $90 million in repairs to rural roads and critical infrastructure (Vantha 2020).

The government has stressed its commitment to improving the flood resilience of road infrastructure through strategic policies and investment priorities. The commitment to more flood-resilient road infrastructure entails promoting investments and enhancing infrastructure to increase flood and drought resilience (MOE, Cambodia, 2013). More than $300 million in financing, mainly from multilateral development banks, has been committed to achieving these goals in collaboration with Cambodia's Ministry of Public Works and Transport (MPWT) and Ministry of Rural Development (MRD). Most infrastructure investment plans are focused on constructing new climate-resilient roads or strengthening existing roads (Table A.2). These financial commitments to resilience underscore the need for mechanisms to help the government consider uncertainties and reduce the risk of maladaptation when planning and implementing road infrastructure projects.

Table A.2: Planned Investments in Road Infrastructure Resilience in Cambodia—MPWT and MRD Projects

Planned Investment	Actions	Cost ($ million)
Rural Roads Improvement Project III (in partnership with ADB)[a]	Refurbish 360 km of roads	40
Road Network Improvement Project (in partnership with ADB)[b]	Strengthen the Greater Mekong Subregion Southern Economic Corridor by improving national roads	70
Cambodia Road Connectivity Improvement Plan (in partnership with the World Bank)[c]	Rehabilitate 380 km of roads for improved connectivity and climate resilience	100
Recovery from 2020 extreme floods (MRD)[d]	Repair 600 roads and related critical infrastructure	91

ADB = Asian Development Bank, km = kilometer, MPWT = Ministry of Public Works and Transport, MRD = Ministry of Rural Development.
Note: This list is based on a literature review of Cambodian infrastructure projects but may not be comprehensive.
[a] MRD, Cambodia (2018).
[b] ADB (n.d.[a]).
[c] World Bank (2020b).
[d] Vantha (2020).
Source: Vivid Economics, based on review of several sources.

The government currently assesses flood risk with the help of an in-house tool for meeting defined resilience objectives. The MPWT framework involves the use of four strategies: repairing and rehabilitating vulnerable road infrastructure, designing new road drainage systems, making broader road networks more adaptive and resilient, and building and strengthening institutions (MPWT, NCSD, and MOE, Cambodia, 2019). The MPWT uses the Flood Risk Management Interface (FRMI), an in-house software, in determining flood risk in an area and the costs of risk adaptation measures (ADB, n.d.[b]). In a recent project assisted by the Asian Development Bank (ADB), the FRMI facilitated the preliminary screening of road flood risk and the preparation of a flood risk map that was later used in prioritizing investments under the project (MRD, Cambodia, 2018).

---

[2]   National one-digit roads are major roads connecting to Phnom Penh. National two-digit roads are other important roads that are maintained by the national government instead of the provincial/local governments.

With better risk information, decision-making in Cambodia would improve. Additional information relevant to risk assessment would improve FRMI-assisted resource allocation and investment decision-making. For example, a more comprehensive analysis of the socioeconomic impact of road closure could clarify the costs of flooding and facilitate investment prioritization. The interface could also be improved with data on rural roads and a more granular evaluation of flood risk (MRD, Cambodia, 2018).[3] In other words, there is a need for an approach that considers the full range of uncertainties in road risk assessment, and in the use of roads by future populations.

Step-by-Step Approach: Adaptive Pathways for Infrastructure Resilience

This subsection outlines a step-by-step approach to developing DAPP for enhancing infrastructure resilience in response to climate risk uncertainties. There are three main analytical steps in the development of an adaptive pathway. These steps and the output achieved after each step are presented in Figure A.2.

- **Objective setting and long-listing of options.** In this first phase, the objectives, parameters, and outputs of the pathway analysis are set, and the intervention options are combined into a long list of pathway options for achieving the objectives.

- **Appraisal of options.** The appraisal phase starts by identifying the relevant cost and benefit categories, before developing adequate quantification methodologies for comparing the costs and benefits of the different pathways.

- **Strategic planning.** The last phase provides an approach to pathway selection.

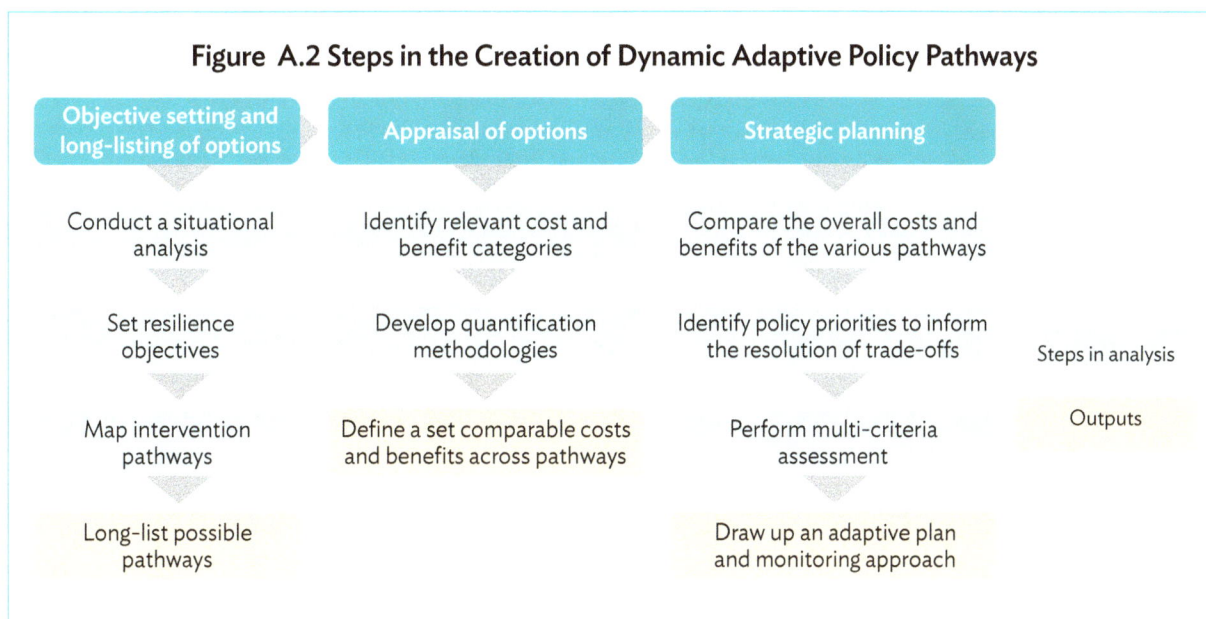

Figure A.2 Steps in the Creation of Dynamic Adaptive Policy Pathways

Objective setting and long-listing of options	Appraisal of options	Strategic planning	
Conduct a situational analysis	Identify relevant cost and benefit categories	Compare the overall costs and benefits of the various pathways	
Set resilience objectives	Develop quantification methodologies	Identify policy priorities to inform the resolution of trade-offs	Steps in analysis
Map intervention pathways	Define a set comparable costs and benefits across pathways	Perform multi-criteria assessment	Outputs
Long-list possible pathways		Draw up an adaptive plan and monitoring approach	

Source: Vivid Economics.

---

3 The current interface has a resolution of 90 meters (m). A model with a 30 m resolution is being developed.

Phase 1: Objective setting and long-listing of options

The objective of the first phase is to gather relevant information and make key decisions that are needed to formulate the pathways. A well-defined context, risk assessment, and objective is a prerequisite for the effective application of the DAPP approach. The situational analysis should be informed by a participatory process and consultation with key stakeholders where possible.

A situational analysis enables an understanding of the broader decision-making and risk context and the definition of resilience objectives. The situational analysis supports the identification of DAPP priorities, focus, and requirements. Key reference points for identifying these in the situational analysis are as follows:

- **The asset or area of focus.** This definition can be informed by a spatial analysis of risks and vulnerabilities, and projections of population and economic growth that may indicate the location of future infrastructure investments. Stakeholder engagement, to understand priorities and their alignment with policy objectives or with planned infrastructure investments, may also be helpful.

- **The range of hazards and the vulnerability of the asset to these hazards.** This definition can be informed by physical risk projections.[4] The findings of this analysis can be used iteratively in defining DAPP goals and the risks the pathways should address.

- **Key socioeconomic uncertainties.** Socioeconomic uncertainty refers to uncertainty around population, job growth, or other social/economic outcomes that may affect the value, use, or location of assets. This uncertainty must be taken into account in defining the DAPP, as socioeconomic uncertainties affect the costs and benefits of resilience strategies. Established socioeconomic scenarios like the Shared Socioeconomic Pathways, which present a range of possible future conditions related to population and economic growth (IIASA, n.d.), can help in understanding key socioeconomic uncertainties. Local knowledge and stakeholder engagement could also provide supplementary information.

- **Strategic priorities of local stakeholders.** In order to be effective determinants of the direction and focus of decision-making, as well as its outcomes, the DAPP must provide information that aligns with existing decision-making processes. After the key decision makers are identified, the information they need to manage the identified risks fully should be identified, through consultation.

The next step is to define measurable resilience objectives to govern the pathways. A resilience objective is a threshold that all defined pathways must meet at any given point in time. This could be an objective stated in policy, a fixed amount of damage that can be sustained, or any other measurable goal of investing in resilience. The resilience objective determines the sets of options available to decision makers, as the DAPP assemble sequenced interventions that will meet the objective under future risk conditions.

- **Resilience objectives.** If DAPP are focused on an asset, a review of the literature on risk management standards and consultations with local stakeholders would improve understanding of key needs and objectives. For example, the resilience objective for the present case study is flood protection from a 1-in-100-year flood event. This objective was arrived at following a review of road resilience design documents published by ADB and the government, which highlighted this objective as a road design standard.

- **Thresholds for measuring resilience objectives.** To develop the pathway, each intervention is assessed against the resilience objective to determine when further investment is required. The metrics for measuring resilience objectives could be based on return periods, losses, damage, a measure of severity, or a combination of criteria by return period. The metrics selected are likely to be limited by data availability and dictated by the needs of decision makers.

---

[4]   Examples of physical risk modeling can be found in Section 4.

Next, the scope of the analysis is set. Key decisions are involved:

- **Unit of spatial analysis.** The unit of spatial analysis for the DAPP is the level of detail that the interventions will address, such as a specific asset (e.g., a bridge) or a specific region (e.g., a city). The unit of spatial analysis for the pathway will be based on the area of interest and the goals of the DAPP. The smaller the unit of spatial analysis, the more specific the DAPP will be in terms of the overall interventions. For example, in the case study described in this appendix, the unit of spatial analysis selected is a specific road segment. Choosing a particular road segment for use in the spatial analysis, instead of an entire highway, enables the DAPP interventions to focus on specific solutions for the identified road segment. More general solutions, on the other hand, may be more applicable to a larger asset.

- **Temporal scope.** Temporal scope refers to the timescale of the pathway, which includes both the duration of the pathway (e.g., 100 years) and the points at which risk is assessed (e.g., every 10 years). An appropriate temporal scope must be defined because it will affect the timing of a switch to new adaptive actions, according to the DAPP and based on changes in flood risk. The definition of temporal scope, however, is likely to be constrained by data availability; for example, the DAPP in the Cambodia case study is limited to flood risk information from the present up to 2080, with data points for risk in 2030, 2050, and 2080. In the definition, therefore, a careful balance must be sought between having enough information to develop a comprehensive pathway and adding too much complexity for the pathway to be useful in decision-making. The length of the pathway may also be informed by links to policy goals; for example, achieving a particular level of resilience by 2040 could be a policy objective.

- **Decision risk metrics.** Decision risk metrics are quantitative measures that represent the risk of an investment or action. Expected annual damage, which uses the probability of events occurring in a given year to calculate the probability-weighted expected damage to an asset, is one example. These metrics are needed to evaluate the risk associated with different pathway steps.

- **Representation of uncertainty.** Representations of uncertainty refer to the development of a range of scenarios that cover a broad spectrum of climate and socioeconomic risk. These scenarios are important because the DAPP structure and decision points are based on the outcomes of different scenarios. In general, it is recommended that adaptive pathways plan for 2 degrees of global warming while including pathway options for up to 4 degrees of warming to account for a world in which climate risks may become very severe (Environment Agency, United Kingdom, 2021). For example, the Cambodia case study uses two climate scenarios (Representative Concentration Pathway, or RCP, 4.5 and RCP8.5) and three socioeconomic scenarios (Shared Socioeconomic Pathway, or SSP, 1, SSP2, and SSP3) to account for both dimensions of uncertainty. Ideally, these scenarios are created through a participatory process of generating scenarios or scenario wedges, employing both expert and stakeholder feedback. Data granularity limitations are likely to affect the level of uncertainty that can be considered in a pathway.

The next step is to develop a pathway map by applying the parameters set out in the previous steps.
Each pathway comprises a combination of interventions that can be deployed to meet the resilience criteria. The sequence is informed by tipping points (thresholds at which current levels of investment and adaptation no longer meet resilience criteria) and trigger points (outside events that prompt decision makers to make specific decisions or to hedge against the occurrence of a tipping point). "Optioneering" identifies candidate interventions, defines tipping points at which an individual intervention can no longer meet the resilience objective across scenarios, and maps out all feasible combinations of interventions (pathways) that can achieve the resilience objective.

- **Candidate interventions that can build resilience to the risk.** Candidate interventions are actions that a decision maker can take to mitigate or address some vulnerabilities of the asset to risk. These interventions can be hard (e.g., physical infrastructure enhancements, forest / green space restoration) and/or soft (e.g., early warning systems, spatial and land use planning).

- **Fitness for purpose of the candidate interventions.** Besides directly addressing the resilience criteria, the candidate interventions must be both technologically and financially feasible. The extent to which the interventions are fit-for-purpose should be assessed, ideally with stakeholder input. If there are many options, this assessment process could involve the long-listing and short-listing of candidates based on efficacy, cost, or other criteria. While a larger number of candidates results in more pathways and greater pathway flexibility, there is a trade-off between full (and often overly complex) pathway coverage and clarity of decision inputs.

- **Key trigger points for the asset. Key trigger points are decision deadlines.** Decisions surrounding the asset's vulnerabilities must be made at those points, to enable hedging against risk by going with a different intervention to meet resilience objectives before a tipping point is reached. In effect, the pathway branches off at the trigger point. These points may be identified through spatial vulnerability analysis using future projections of physical hazard data, or through consultation with experts, but the identification process may be limited by the granularity of data available. A lag period of action—the amount of time available to a decision maker to implement an intervention after a trigger point is reached, to prevent damage to the asset / area of interest—can be defined. This definition can be based on the speed at which a vulnerability can develop, and decision makers can mobilize. As a rule of thumb, 5 years is generally considered sufficient time to prepare for an impending tipping point, and to adapt and react to that expected occurrence.

- **Preliminary pathway map, showing trigger points and candidate interventions.** The map traces the sequence of actions to be taken over time as climate conditions change. It defines a base plan of action and identifies the points in time at which new information about the climate scenario should be reviewed. Given this information, it then determines the actions that should be taken to ensure that resilience objectives continue to be met.

Phase 2: Appraisal of Options

In addition to meeting resilience criteria, policy makers may have a wider set of objectives. These can be taken into account in the appraisal of pathway options, to allow decision makers to prioritize the pathways to follow. The appraisal can be done in five steps (Figure A.3), leading to the selection of the most suitable pathway and the development of an adaptive plan.

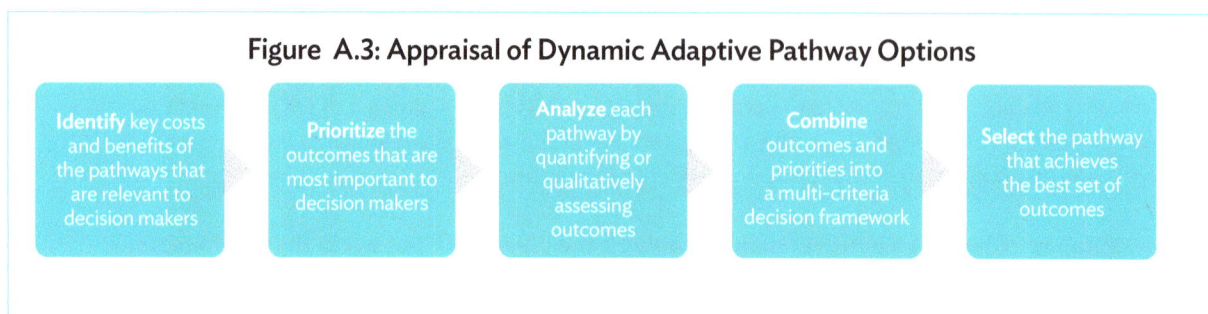

Figure A.3: Appraisal of Dynamic Adaptive Pathway Options

Identify key costs and benefits of the pathways that are relevant to decision makers → **Prioritize** the outcomes that are most important to decision makers → **Analyze** each pathway by quantifying or qualitatively assessing outcomes → **Combine** outcomes and priorities into a multi-criteria decision framework → **Select** the pathway that achieves the best set of outcomes

Source: Vivid Economics.

The first step is to identify the types of costs and benefits of each pathway that are important to decision makers. The costs can include capital expenditure or labor costs related to the implementation of the adaptive strategy. The benefits, on the other hand, can include direct benefits (e.g., averted damage costs), indirect benefits (e.g., social benefits to local communities), and co-benefits of specific interventions (e.g., nature-based solutions).

Once key costs and benefits have been identified, the next step is to develop a methodology for assessment. Ideally, the methodology will monetize all costs and benefits where possible to put outcomes into standardized units, quantify additional outcomes where not possible to monetize, and qualitatively assess all other outcomes. For example, the Cambodian road case study assesses the outcomes of the pathways through a combination of monetized benefits (avoided expected annual damage[5]) and quantified benefits (estimated population at risk where roads are unsurpassable due to flooding[6]). Sample methodologies for quantifying and monetizing the benefits of resilient infrastructure investments were shown in Table 6.

Phase 3: Strategic Planning

The assessment framework can be used in selecting an adaptive pathway based on stakeholder priorities. The assessed costs and benefits can be combined into a multi-criteria assessment (MCA) framework, also referred to as a balanced scorecard approach. The MCA framework provides a structured way of comparing options by combining qualitative and quantitative data. The assessment results in a performance matrix, which summarizes information about outcomes against stated criteria. The outcomes can then be weighted on the basis of stakeholder priorities and objectives.

Once a pathway has been selected, it can be institutionalized with a monitoring and evaluation plan to update the pathway as additional information about climate and socioeconomic risk becomes available. Key considerations to cover in the monitoring and evaluation plan include: sensitivities of the assumptions made for the pathways, a clear time frame for the periodic review of the pathway, and assurance that pathway actions will be implemented as sequenced.

Application to Flood-Resilient Roads in Cambodia

The objective of this case study is to demonstrate how using a DAPP approach could inform decision-making in Cambodia. This approach is most useful when there is a high degree of uncertainty, or significant variation in the outcomes of the choices that decision makers face. The case study shows that the approach can build a knowledge base of risks and opportunities and provide a clear adaptation strategy, even amid limited uncertainty.

The DAPP approach makes a strong case for early action—a point not commonly highlighted in standard investment appraisal tools. Key findings from the DAPP analysis include the following:

- **Low-regret action is possible in the short term.** Under a standard approach, decision makers may prefer to delay action until climate outcomes are more certain. However, the DAPP analysis shows that early action can protect roads over the short term as well as the medium term. The year 2050 is highlighted as a key point for reassessing risk.

- **Incremental action may be less cost-effective.** If resources are limited, decision makers may prefer to invest incrementally in resilience. The DAPP analysis, however, shows that early action, while marginally more expensive in the short term, is much more cost-effective in the long term and provides greater protection across climate scenarios. For one of the road segments analyzed, early investment could lead to total savings of more than $600,000 when compared with investing in four increments.

- **Accounting for non-monetizable benefits can strengthen the case for early investment in resilience.** When only averted damage is considered, most of the pathways assessed yield low benefit–cost ratios. This suggests

---

[5]   The same methodology implemented previously in Cambodia (code and data available).
[6]   The same methodology used in critical infrastructure mapping done previously for Cambodia and Pakistan (code and data available).

that decision makers using standard appraisal tools could delay investments in resilience. However, a key benefit of road resilience is maintaining road access for vulnerable populations and economic activity. In the preferred pathways, investments in resilience improvements are made earlier in view of these outcomes.

Approach

Building road resilience in Cambodia is critical to maintaining economic activity but made challenging by climate and socioeconomic uncertainty. As discussed earlier in this section, economic activity in Cambodia depends highly on national arterial roads that connect the northern and southern regions of the country and link to the wider Mekong region. However, two key uncertainties complicate investment decisions:

- **Climate uncertainty.** Cambodia is already highly flood-affected, but the degree to which flooding will increase in the future is uncertain. In most countries, more extreme climate change is associated with greater flooding. However, previous analysis has shown that Cambodia experiences less flooding in more extreme climate change scenarios (RCP8.5) because of drought conditions.

- **Socioeconomic uncertainty.** Cambodia's population is currently concentrated in the capital regions, but it is uncertain where future population and economic growth will occur. For example, SSP3 shows growth concentrated in areas in the capital with access to the sea and existing infrastructure, while SSP1 shows growth that is more concentrated in the north. The importance of roads linking the regions depends on the dispersion of the population and economic activity.

As a result, decision makers need an approach that covers the range of possible futures while avoiding maladaptation of infrastructure. The DAPP approach supports decision makers in identifying short-term low-regret options with clearly identified tipping points, when hedging options can be considered as better information becomes more available in the future.

This analysis is focused on three road segments that are important for the internal flow of goods and services. The selection of these road segments was based on a spatial analysis of the distribution of flood depths to which road segments are exposed across different climate change scenarios, as well as the variance in flood depths. The three road segments, each one at least 4 km long, were identified as representative of key flood dynamics faced by arterial roads in Cambodia. Implementing ad-hoc emergency solutions in these segments would result in flooding that is more costly, disruptive, and challenging. Building resilience is likely to be more important.

Population growth under three socioeconomic projection scenarios was also analyzed to enable the selection of critical road segments. Already important arterial roads across all socioeconomic scenarios, these road segments will provide vital protection from flood risk when socioeconomic growth occurs in the north and it becomes increasingly necessary to link the northern and southern regions. The road segments used in the analysis are shown in Map 5.

Map 5: Key Road Segments in Cambodia

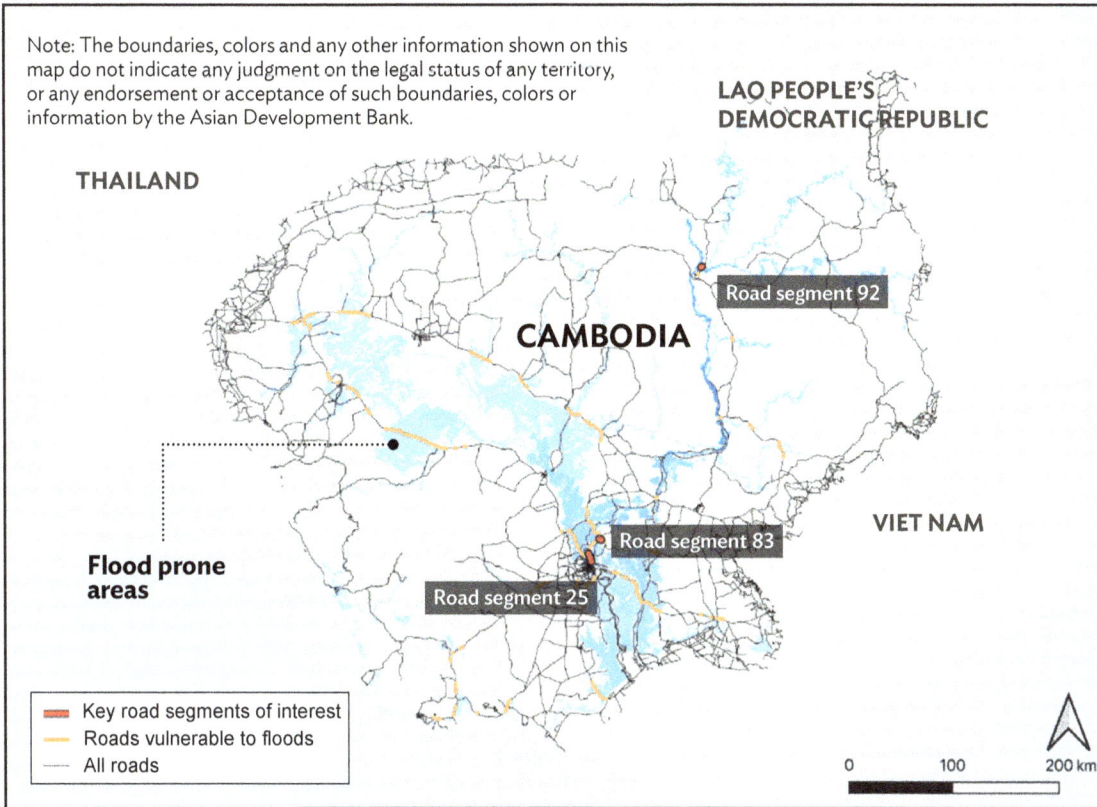

Note: The boundaries, colors and any other information shown on this map do not indicate any judgment on the legal status of any territory, or any endorsement or acceptance of such boundaries, colors or information by the Asian Development Bank.

THAILAND

LAO PEOPLE'S DEMOCRATIC REPUBLIC

CAMBODIA

Road segment 92

VIET NAM

Road segment 83

Road segment 25

Flood prone areas

Key road segments of interest

Roads vulnerable to floods

All roads

0   100   200 km

Source: https://greatermekong.org/content/economic-corridors-in-the-greater-mekong-subregion.

The pathways assess the timing and sequence of investments in embankment height raising. The effectiveness of road-raising and road-paving interventions against flood risk in Cambodia is often brought out in the academic literature and policy documents. Incremental increases in embankment height were selected as the interventions of focus in the case study because these can be easily mapped to flood depth protection and sufficient cost data were available. Road paving was not considered among the potential interventions because all national roads in Cambodia are already paved. The cost of incremental height raising was based on estimates from the Rural Roads Improvement Project, extrapolated to the increments and slopes required for the road segments analyzed by fitting the cost data to a natural log function. Costs (and monetized benefits) incurred in the future were discounted at an annual discount rate of 11%.

Key Parameters of the Analysis in the National Adaptation Plan

In the decision context phase of the analysis, three key analytical constraints were selected:

- **Resilience objective.** The threshold for resilience used in the analysis was road asset protection from the depth of flooding in a 1-in-100-year flood event. This threshold was selected on the basis of prior government risk assessments showing that it affords a reasonable level of protection, as these events are rare. This objective was adjusted in line with climate change, to maintain 1-in-100-year flooding even with more frequent flood events.

- **Temporal scale.** Risk of flooding, as well as its impact, at present (2020), and in 2030, 2050, and 2080, was analyzed. The analysis was limited by the availability of data on future flood risk.

- **Uncertainties considered.** Climate uncertainty is characterized by two RCPs representing intermediate and worst-case levels of emissions and associated temperature increases (RCP4.5 and RCP8.5, respectively); socioeconomic uncertainty, by three SSPs representing inclusive and sustainable development, development consistent with historical patterns, and persistent inequality (SSP1, SSP2, and SSP3, respectively). Climate uncertainty affects the flood frequency and depth experienced at the road segments, while socioeconomic uncertainty affects population and GDP at risk when flooding makes roads impassable.[a]

GDP = gross domestic product, RCP = Representative Concentration Pathway, SSP = Shared Socioeconomic Pathway.
[a] The terms "Representative Concentration Pathway (RCP)" and "Shared Socioeconomic Pathway (SSP)" are defined in IPCC (2014).
Source: IPCC (2014).

The pathways were scored against three types of costs and benefits: averted road damage, averted traffic slowdown, and remaining population and GDP at risk. Averted road damage was estimated using global flood depth–damage functions (Huizinga, de Moel, and Szewczyk 2017) and Cambodia-specific data on road reconstruction costs (World Bank, n.d.[a]). Calculations of traffic disruption along flooded, but still passable, roads were based on time lost from the slowdown in freight vehicles. A spatial analysis of the population and GDP within a radius of road segments made impassable by flooding was used in estimating the remaining population and GDP at risk, to serve as proxy for the population that may be unable to evacuate during extreme flooding, and for economic activity that may be unable to continue. Averted road damage and traffic disruption benefits vary by climate future; population and GDP at risk, by socioeconomic future.

Findings from the Analysis

The analysis indicates that the asset can be protected against 1-in-100-year flooding through four sequences of actions. The sequences are based on combinations of the following actions:

- The minimum level of action required in the short term is to raise the embankment to a level of protection against 1-in-100-year flooding.

- An intermediate level of action would be to raise the embankment by 0.3 m.

- The highest level of action would involve raising the embankment by 1 m.

The pathway map highlights 2050 as a key decision point. Figure A.4 below lays out the sequence of embankment height raising against the tipping points across two climate scenarios. The map shows that any initial action taken in the short term provides protection until at least 2050, when the tipping point is reached in RCP4.5. The pathway map also shows that the outcomes diverge significantly between the climate scenarios from 2050 onward: over the long term, tipping points are reached more quickly in RCP4.5 because RCP8.5 leads to more drought-like conditions with less rainfall. Accordingly, actions taken before 2050 leave little scope for regret. Climatic conditions by 2050 can be reassessed with the help of a robust monitoring plan to arrive at a better understanding of likely climate outcomes.

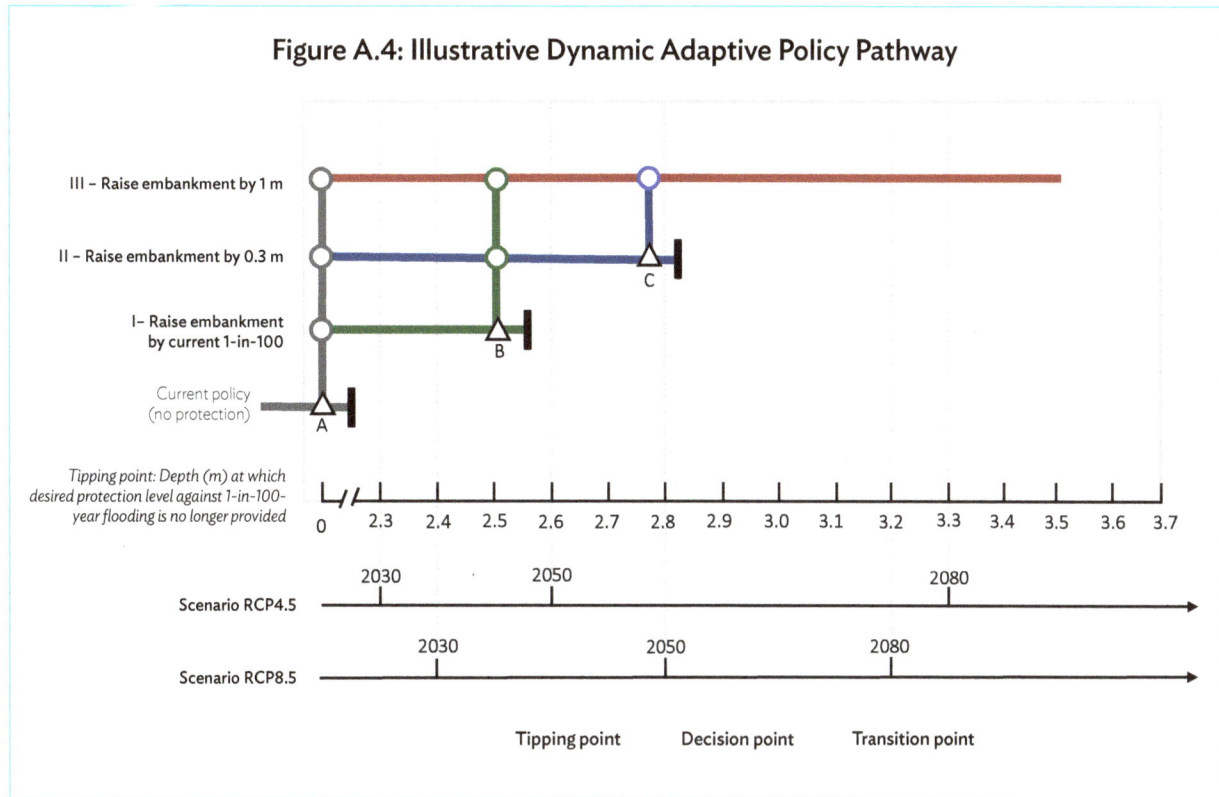

Figure A.4: Illustrative Dynamic Adaptive Policy Pathway

Source: Vivid Economics.

Across most road segments, immediate investment in the highest level of protection is the most favorable option. Immediate high-level action lowers the investment cost significantly across road segments. For road segment 92, considered in Figure A.6, the cost is three to nine times greater for intervention pathways other than immediate maximum action. Monetized benefits do not vary widely across pathways. For instance, in segment 92, the monetized benefits from immediate maximum action are higher than those for other pathways under SSP1 in both climate scenarios, and represent over 95% of the maximum possible benefits under other socioeconomic scenarios (Figure A.5). The non-monetized benefits are highest for the pathway with immediate maximum action; this means that the pathway ensures protection for as many people and as much GDP as possible.

Figure A.5: Investment Cost for Road Segment 92, by Pathway

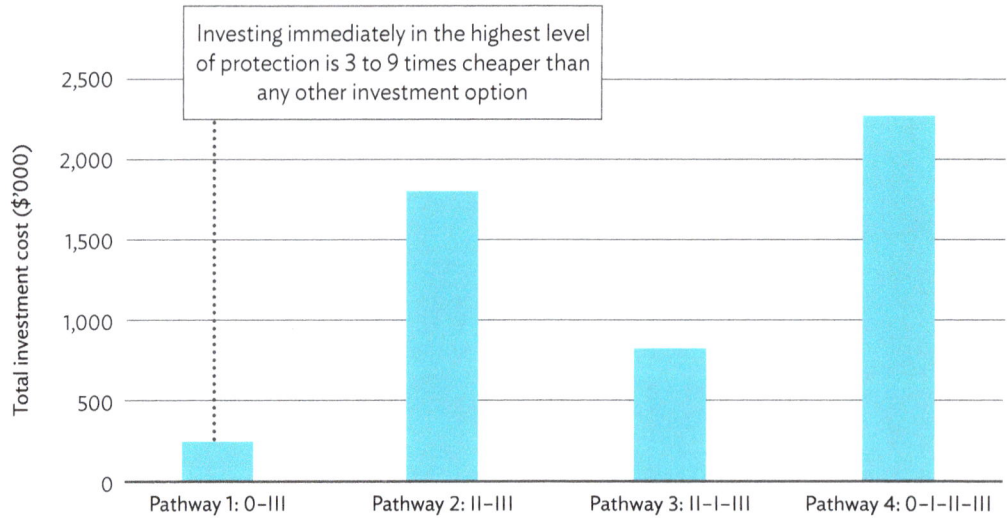

Investing immediately in the highest level of protection is 3 to 9 times cheaper than any other investment option

Total investment cost ($'000)

2,500

2,000

1,500

1,000

500

0

Pathway 1: 0–III | Pathway 2: II–III | Pathway 3: II–I–III | Pathway 4: 0–I–II–III

Source: Vivid Economics.

Figure A.6: Monetized Annual Benefit in 2050 for Road Segment 92, by Intervention Pathway and by Climate and Socioeconomic Scenario

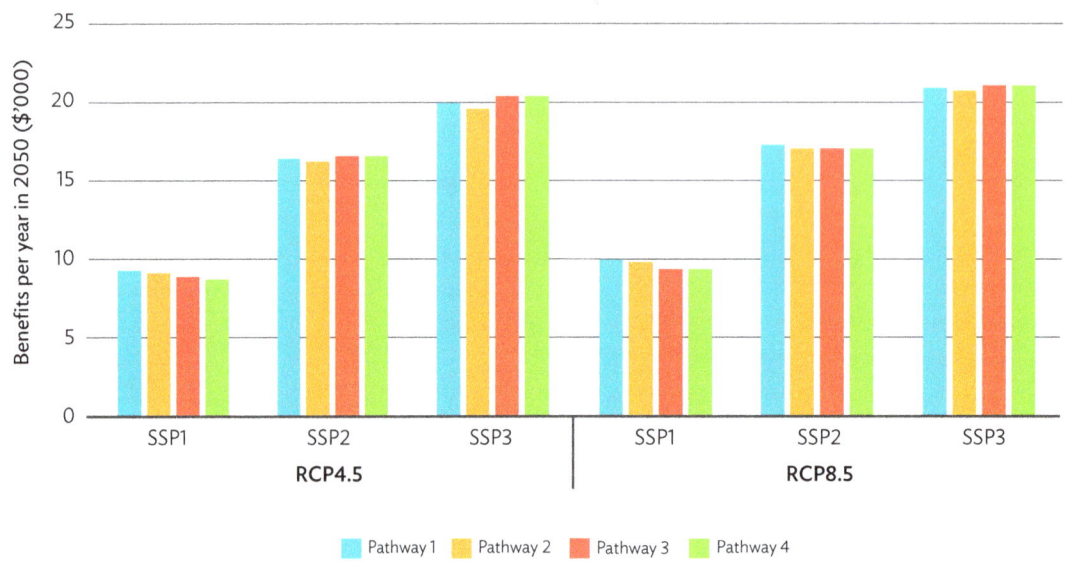

Benefits per year in 2050 ($'000)

25

20

15

10

5

0

SSP1 | SSP2 | SSP3 | SSP1 | SSP2 | SSP3

RCP4.5 | RCP8.5

Pathway 1 Pathway 2 Pathway 3 Pathway 4

RCP = Representative Concentration Pathway, SSP = Shared Socioeconomic Pathway.
Source: Vivid Economics.

For some road segments, low-regret action is possible in the short term. Typically, the investments with the highest level of protection are also the highest-cost. Therefore, using standard investment appraisal tools may keep decision makers from investing in high-cost action until climate risks are more certain. However, because there is limited variation in flood risk between the climate scenarios and because the resilience objective demands a high level of protection, all of the pathways offer similar benefits. Therefore, investing in the maximum level of feasible protection in the short term (pathway 1) may be the most cost-effective action for these road segments in Cambodia. A traditional appraisal approach, in contrast, may result in minimal action in the short term, thus increasing the total costs incurred by the government.

Table A.3: Optimal Pathways for Key Road Segments in Cambodia

Item	Road Segment		
	25	83	92
Characteristics	Part of the important National Road 6A connecting the capital of Phnom Penh to the northwestern provinces of Banteay Meanchey and Siem Reap. North–south movement of goods and services between the airports at Siem Reap and Phnom Penh depends on this segment with no other bypass.	Important section of National Road 8 connecting the capital city to the southeastern province of Prey Veng, and a trading route that continues into the vital Vung Tau seaport of Viet Nam.	Important section of National Road 7 without any bypass that connects the northeastern provinces with the capital city, and part of the Asia Highway Network that connects further to the Lao People's Democratic Republic, Thailand, and Viet Nam.
Optimal pathway	Investing in the maximum protection is the most cost-effective pathway. This covers risks both for short-term and long-term futures across all RCPs and SSPs.	Pathway 1 provides the highest level of annual monetizable benefits relative to investment costs, but pathway 3 provides better protection from extreme flood events in the medium term (2050).	

RCP = Representative Concentration Pathway, SSP = Shared Socioeconomic Pathway.
Source: Vivid Economics.

Pathways with incremental action, where the embankment is raised in several phases, are more expensive in aggregate but may still be preferred by key stakeholders. Raising embankments to the minimum level differs only marginally in cost per kilometer from raising them to the maximum level. For example, for road segment 25, investing in the lowest embankment option, rather than the highest (with a total cost of $1.8 million), saves only $12,000 per kilometer. But when considered as a whole over time, incremental pathways are significantly more expensive in this example, even when costs incurred in the future are discounted. Spreading the cost over time may, however, still be preferred if there are competing stakeholder priorities, if resources are very limited, or if the road requiring protection is very long. For other examples, the aggregate cost over time may compare very differently. In particular, in instances with more variability in future risk across the range of scenarios analyzed, the aggregate cost over time may be notably lower for incremental pathways, as there is reduced risk of early maladaptation and an associated increase in costs later on.

The adaptive pathways approach and multi-criteria analysis highlight the importance of accounting for non-monetizable benefits. Failing to consider non-monetizable benefits may underestimate the investment case for resilience if traditional appraisal tools are used, and affect the selection of the preferred pathway. These benefits can have long-term development implications but are more challenging to monetize. When only the benefits from averted road damage costs and time savings from averted traffic slowdowns are considered, most of the pathways assessed yield low benefit–cost ratios. However, a key benefit of road resilience is maintaining road access for vulnerable populations that may require shelter during extreme events. Road infrastructure is also important for continued access to health and humanitarian services. This case study assesses non-monetizable benefits in the appraisal stage, but an approach with a different resilience objective (e.g., to minimize the population exposed to flood risk) could place even greater emphasis on these outcomes; this approach could determine tipping points for action based on variation in socioeconomic futures.

A lower-resilience objective may lead to different preferred pathways. For this analysis, a very high level of road protection was selected as the resilience criterion on the basis of policy priorities. Since the risk of flooding exceeding this threshold is limited (<1% chance in any given year) and the intervention options do not have different co-benefits, there are limited differences in the benefits achieved by the pathways. The most cost-effective pathway is therefore the preferred option. However, when the resilience threshold is lowered to protection against 1-in-25-year flood events, pathways with fewer increments are not always preferred. For road segment 25, there is more variation in the population and GDP at risk when the resilience objective is lowered. When the resilience objective is high, all pathways offer protection for the population and GDP at risk and the preferred pathways are based on cost efficiency. With a lower resilience threshold, pathway 2 leaves 1.9–2.2 million people at risk by 2050 in both climate scenarios. By comparison, pathway 2 is less cost-efficient on monetizable benefits, but protects against road closures in 2050 and minimizes the population and GDP at risk.

The case study demonstrates that a deep understanding of uncertainties can lead to more cost-effective action, even when uncertainty is limited. The pathways developed for the national roads in Cambodia demonstrate that because of limited variation in flood risk between climate futures, there is limited risk of maladaptation and therefore few trade-offs to resolve in achieving a high level of flood resilience. The pathways therefore highlight a straightforward approach and low-regret investments for achieving road resilience. The process of developing robust pathways forces decision makers to develop a comprehensive understanding of risks and uncertainties, and to prioritize resilience objectives.

Glossary

This section gives an overview of key terms used in this report and their definitions. The definitions describe how each term is used in this report. They are not intended to provide a holistic description of each concept, but instead represent the idealized view adopted specifically for the purposes of the report.

Infrastructure system. An interconnected network of infrastructure assets within and across different sectors, whose successful delivery of services to users relies on the overall functioning of the entire system.

Geophysical hazard. A hazard originating from internal earth processes. Examples are earthquakes, volcanic activity and emissions, and related geophysical processes, such as mass movements, landslides, rockslides, surface collapse, and debris or mudflows.

Climate hazard. A hazard of atmospheric, hydrologic, or oceanographic origin. Examples are tropical cyclones (also known as typhoons or hurricanes), floods (including flash floods), drought, heat waves and cold spells, and coastal storm surges.

Natural hazard. A geophysical or climate hazard, as defined above.

Exposure. Assets, people, and economic capacities located in hazard-prone areas (UNDRR, n.d.[b]).

Vulnerability. Conditions determined by physical, social, economic, and environmental factors or processes that make infrastructure assets, networks, or users more susceptible to the impact of hazards (UNDRR, n.d.[b]).[1]

Disaster impact. The direct and indirect effects of a specific disaster on assets, people, and economies. Direct impact includes physical damage and injury. Indirect impact includes the cascading effects on the economy and society, for example, a reduction in economic activity resulting from the inability to gain access to infrastructure services.

Disaster risk. The magnitude of the expected impact of disasters from a given hazard, taking into account their potential to cause impact of varying severity, and the likelihood of their occurrence. Disaster risk is often measured in terms of the expected annual loss, which is the magnitude of loss a particular hazard is expected to cause in a year, on a long-term average.

Long-term stress. Any factor that alters hazards, exposure, vulnerability, or impact over time. Long-term stresses can lead to changes in disaster risk and impact but can also pose a chronic stress in the absence of disasters. Examples are rising sea levels and changes in the location of assets or population (e.g., urbanization).

Resilience. The ability of a system, community, or society exposed to hazards to resist, absorb, accommodate, adapt to, transform, and recover from the effects of a hazard in a timely and efficient manner, through risk management, to preserve and restore its essential basic structures and functions, or through other means (UNDRR, n.d.[b]).[1]

---

[1]   Adapted from: UNDRR. Terminology. 2020-2022.

Asset criticality. The importance of an asset within the overall system to which it belongs, considering the extent to which the system, or a significant part of it, relies on the individual asset to function.

Disaster risk management. The application of disaster risk reduction policies and strategies to prevent new disaster risk, reduce existing disaster risk, and manage residual risk, thus helping to strengthen resilience and reduce disaster losses. Disaster risk management actions come in different types:

- **Disaster risk reduction.** The prevention of new disaster risk, and the reduction of existing risk.

- **Disaster preparedness.** The knowledge and capacities developed by governments, response and recovery organizations, communities, and individuals to effectively anticipate, respond to, and recover from the impact of likely, imminent, or current disasters.

- **Disaster response.** Actions taken directly before, during, or immediately after a disaster to save lives, reduce health impact, ensure public safety, and meet the basic subsistence needs of the people affected.

- **Disaster recovery.** The restoration or improvement of livelihoods and health, as well as the economic, physical, social, cultural, and environmental assets, systems, and activities, of a disaster-affected community or society.

Reconstruction. The medium- and long-term rebuilding and sustainable restoration of assets, services, housing, facilities, and livelihoods required for the full functioning of a community or a society affected by a disaster (UNDRR, n.d.[b]).[1]

Disaster risk financing. Funds disbursed in the aftermath of a disaster, to meet emergency response, recovery, and reconstruction needs (Financial Protection Forum 2015).

Infrastructure financing. Funds for building new, or adapting existing, infrastructure assets.

Climate change mitigation. Interventions made to reduce the sources of greenhouse gas emissions and limit global warming (Klein et al. 2007).

Climate change adaptation. Changes in response to actual or expected effects of climate change, to moderate harm or exploit beneficial opportunities (Klein et al. 2007).

Climate financing. Funds—from public, private, or other sources—intended to support mitigation and adaptation actions that will address climate change (UNFCCC, n.d.).

References

Aalto University, Finland. n.d. *Gridded Global Datasets for Gross Domestic Product and Human Development Index over 1990–2015* (accessed May 2021).

Asian Development Bank (ADB). 2011. *Economics of Climate Proofing at the Project Level: Two Pacific Case Studies*. Manila.

———. 2014. *Central Mekong Delta Region Connectivity Project: Rapid Climate Change Threat and Vulnerability Assessment*. Manila.

———. 2015. *Jiangxi Pingxiang Integrated Rural–Urban Infrastructure Development: Final Report*. Consultant's report. Manila (TA 8451-PRC).

———. 2017. *Meeting Asia's Infrastructure Needs*. Manila.

———. 2019a. *Asian Development Outlook (ADO) 2019 Update: Fostering Growth and Inclusion in Asia's Cities*. Manila.

———. 2019b. *Cambodia: Transport Sector Assessment, Strategy, and Road Map*. Manila.

———. 2021a. How ADB is Supporting Tonga's Climate and Disaster Risk Management. Video. 12 November.

———. 2021b. *Key Indicators for Asia and the Pacific 2021*. Manila.

———. 2021c. *A System-Wide Approach for Infrastructure Resilience: Technical Note*. Manila.

———. n.d.[a]. Cambodia Road Network Improvement Project (accessed October 2021).

———. n.d.[b]. Climate Risk Assessment and Management: Road Network Improvement Project in Cambodia (accessed October 2021).

Asian Infrastructure Investment Bank (AIIB). 2019. *Asian Infrastructure Finance 2019. Bridging Borders: Infrastructure to Connect Asia and Beyond*. Beijing.

———. 2020. *Asian Infrastructure Finance: 2020: Investing Better, Investing More*. Beijing.

Browder, Greg, Suzanne Ozment, Irene Rehberger Bescos, Todd Gartner, and Glenn-Marie Lange . 2019. *Integrating Green and Gray: Creating Next Generation Infrastructure*. Washington, DC: World Bank and World Resources Institute.

Centre for Research on the Epidemiology of Disasters (CRED). n.d. EM-DAT: The International Disaster Database (accessed December 2021).

Chausson, Alexandre, Beth Turner, Dan Seddon, Nicole Chabaneix, Cécile A. J. Girardin, Valerie Kapos, Isabel Key, Dilys Roe, Alison Smith, Stephen Woroniecki, and Nathalie Seddon. 2020. Mapping the Effectiveness of Nature-Based Solutions for Climate Change Adaptation. *Global Change Biology*. 26 (11). pp. 6134–6155.

Cheng, Chii-Ming, and Cheng-Hsin Chang. 2009. *APEC-WW2009 Economy Report*. Taipei,China: Wind Engineering Research Center, Tamkang University.

Clarke, Daniel J., and Stefan Dercon. 2016. *Dull Disasters? How Planning Ahead Will Make a Difference*. New York: Oxford University Press.

Dartmouth Flood Observatory (DFO), University of Colorado, USA. n.d. Global Active Archive of Large Flood Events, 1985–Present (accessed December 2021).

Delta Programme Commissioner, Netherlands. 2018. *Delta Programme 2019. Continuing the Work on the Delta: Adapting the Netherlands to Climate Change in Time*. The Hague: Ministry of Agriculture, Nature and Food Quality, and Ministry of the Interior and Kingdom Relations.

Department for Business, Energy and Industrial Strategy (BEIS), United Kingdom. 2021. Future Funding for Nuclear Plants. News story. 26 October. London.

Development Workshop France. n.d. Cyclone Damage Prevention to Housing – Vietnam (accessed December 2021).

Dilley, Maxx, Robert S. Chen, Uwe Deichmann, Arthur L. Lerner-Lam, and Margaret Arnold. 2005. *Natural Disaster Hotspots: A Global Risk Analysis*. Washington, DC: World Bank.

Douven, W. J. A. M., M. Goichot, and H. J. Verheij. 2009. *Roads and Floods: Best Practice Guidelines for the Integrated Planning and Design of Economically Sound and Environmentally Friendly Roads in the Mekong Floodplains of Cambodia and Viet Nam*. Vientiane, Lao People's Democratic Republic: Mekong River Commission.

Economics Online. 2020. Contestability.

Environment Agency, United Kingdom. 2012. *Thames Estuary (TE2100) Plan: Managing Flood Risk through London and the Thames Estuary*. London.

———. 2021. *Delivering Benefits through Evidence: Literature Review on an Adaptive Approach to Flood and Coastal Risk Management*. FRS19221. Bristol.

Espinet Alegre, X., Z. Stanton-Geddes, S. Aliyev, and V. Bun. 2020. Analyzing Flooding Impacts on Rural Access to Hospitals and Other Critical Services in Rural Cambodia Using Geo-Spatial Information and Network Analysis. *Policy Research Working Paper*. No. 9262. Washington, DC: World Bank.

European Bank for Reconstruction and Development (EBRD), African Development Bank (AfDB), Asian Development Bank (ADB), Asian Infrastructure Investment Bank (AIIB), European Investment Bank (EIB), Inter-American Development Bank Group (IDB), Islamic Development Bank (IsDB), New Development Bank (NDB), and World Bank Group (WBG). 2021. *2020 Joint Report on Multilateral Development Banks' Climate Finance*. UK: EBRD.

Evans, Steve. 2022. Philippines Cat Bond Triggers on Typhoon Rai (Odette) Winds, $52.5m Payout Due. www.artemis.bm. 24 January.

Federal Ministry for the Environment, Nature Conservation and Nuclear Safety (BMU), Germany. 2018. Modeling Catastrophes in the Philippines and Bangladesh. International Climate Initiative. Bonn.

Financial Protection Forum. 2015. What Is Disaster Risk Finance (DRF)?

Government of Viet Nam. 2017. *Resolution No. 120/NQ-CP Dated November 17, 2017 of the Government on Sustainable and Climate Resilient Development of the Mekong River Delta*. Ha Noi.

Greater Mekong Subregion (GMS) Secretariat. n.d. Economic Corridors in the Greater Mekong Subregion (accessed December 2021).

Griscom, Bronson W., Justin Adams, Peter W. Ellis, Richard A. Houghton, Guy Lomax, Daniela A. Miteva , William H. Schlesinger, David Shoch, Juha V. Siikamäki, Pete Smith, Peter Woodbury , Chris Zganjar, Allen Blackman, João Campari, Richard T. Conant, Christopher Delgado, Patricia Elias, Trisha Gopalakrishna, Marisa R. Hamsik, Mario Herrero , Joseph Kiesecker, Emily Landis, Lars Laestadius, Sara M. Leavitt, Susan Minnemeyer , Stephen Polasky, Peter Potapov, Francis E. Putz, Jonathan Sanderman, Marcel Silvius, Eva Wollenberg, and Joseph Fargione. 2017. Natural Climate Solutions. *Proceedings of the National Academy of Sciences* (PNAS). 114 (44). 11645–11650.

Haasnoot, Marjolijn, Jan H. Kwakkel, Warren E. Walker, and Judith ter Maat. 2013. Dynamic Adaptive Policy Pathways: A Method for Crafting Robust Decisions for a Deeply Uncertain World. Global Environmental Change. 23 (2). pp. 485–498.

Hall, Jim. 2021. Informing Decisions about Disaster Resilient Infrastructure Systems … Everywhere. Blog. 24 February. New Delhi: Coalition for Disaster Resilient Infrastructure.

Hallegatte, Stephane, Jun Rentschler, and Julie Rozenberg. 2019. *Lifelines: The Resilient Infrastructure Opportunity*. Washington, DC: World Bank.

Huizinga, Jan, Hans de Moel, and Wojciech Szewczyk. 2017. *Global Flood Depth-Damage Functions: Methodology and the Database with Guidelines*. EUR 28552 EN. Luxembourg: Publications Office of the European Union.

Humanitarian Data Exchange (HDX). n.d.[a]. HOTOSM. Pakistan Education Facilities (accessed 29 March 2021).

———. n.d. [b]. HOTOSM. Pakistan Health Facilities (accessed 24 February 2022).

———. n.d. [c]. HOTOSM. Pakistan Roads (Open Street Map) (accessed 17 February 2022).

Intergovernmental Panel on Climate Change (IPCC). 2014. *Climate Change 2014: Synthesis Report. Contribution of Working Groups I, II and III to the Fifth Assessment Report of the Intergovernmental Panel on Climate Change.* Geneva.

———. 2021. *Climate Change 2021: The Physical Science Basis*. Geneva.

———. n.d. IPCC Working Group I Interactive Atlas (accessed December 2021).

International Institute for Applied Systems Analysis (IIASA). n.d. SSP Database (Shared Socioeconomic Pathways) – Version 2.0 (accessed 17 February 2022).

Klein, R. J. T., S. Huq, F. Denton, T. E. Downing, R. G. Richels, J. B. Robinson, and F. L. Toth. 2007. Inter-relationships between Adaptation and Mitigation. In M. L. Parry, O. F. Canziani , J. P. Palutikof, P. J. van der Linden, and C. E. Hanson, eds., *Climate Change 2007: Impacts, Adaptation and Vulnerability. Contribution of Working Group II to the Fourth Assessment Report of the Intergovernmental Panel on Climate Change.* UK: Cambridge University Press.

Kornejew, Martin, Jun Rentschler, and Stephane Hallegatte. 2019. Well Spent: How Governance Determines the Effectiveness of Infrastructure Investments. Policy Research Working Paper. No. 8894. Washington, DC: World Bank.

Kwakkel, J. H., W. E. Walker, and V. A. W. J. Marchau. 2010. Adaptive Airport Strategic Planning. *European Journal of Transport and Infrastructure Research*. 10 (3). pp. 249–273.

Leng Heng An. 2014. *Country Report of Cambodia Disaster Management*. Kobe: Asian Disaster Reduction Center.

Lloyd's. 2019. *Innovative Finance for Resilient Infrastructure: Four Mechanisms to Incentivise Investment in Resilience*. London.

Lu, Xianfu. 2019. Building Resilient Infrastructure for the Future: Background Paper for the G20 Climate Sustainability Working Group. *ADB Sustainable Development Working Paper Series*. No. 61. Manila: ADB.

Magdoff, Fred. 2007. Ecological Agriculture: Principles, Practices, and Constraints. *Renewable Agriculture and Food Systems*. 22 (2). pp. 109–117.

Mallick, Fuad Hassan, M. Aminur Rahman, Tahmina Rahman, Mohammad Rezaur Rahman, and M. Shahjahan Mondal. 2010. A Comparative Analysis of Different Types of Flood Shelters in Bangladesh. Dhaka: Department of Architecture, BRAC University.

Maxwell, Simon, Davina Henderson, Rachel McCloy, and Gemma Harper. 2011. Social Impacts and Wellbeing: Multi-criteria Analysis Techniques for Integrating Non-monetary Evidence in Valuation and Appraisal. *Defra Evidence and Analysis Series*. Paper 5. London: Department for Environment, Food and Rural Affairs.

Mechler, Reinhard, and Stefan Hochrainer-Stigler. 2019. Generating Multiple Resilience Dividends from Managing Unnatural Disasters in Asia. *ADB Economic Working Paper Series*. No. 601. Manila: Asian Development Bank.

Ministry of Environment (MOE), Cambodia. 2013. *Cambodia Climate Change Strategic Plan 2014–2023*. Phnom Penh.

———. 2017. *National Environment Strategy and Action Plan 2016–2023*. Phnom Penh.

Ministry of Natural Resources and Environment (MONRE) and Ministry of Agriculture and Rural Development (MARD), Viet Nam, and Government of the Netherlands. 2013. *Mekong Delta Plan: Long-Term Vision and Strategy for a Safe, Prosperous and Sustainable Delta*. Hanoi.

Ministry of Public Works and Transport (MPWT), National Council for Sustainable Development (NCSD), and Ministry of Environment (MOE), Cambodia. 2019. *Green Infrastructure Guide*. Phnom Penh.

Ministry of Rural Development (MRD), Cambodia. 2018. *Project Climate and Disaster Risk Assessment: Rural Roads Improvement Project III in Cambodia* (prepared for ADB).

Moss, Anna, and Suzanne Martin. 2012. *Flexible Adaptation Pathways*. Edinburgh, Scotland: ClimateXChange.

Narayan, Siddharth, Michael W. Beck, Borja G. Reguero, Iñigo J. Losada, Bregie van Wesenbeeck , Nigel Pontee, James N. Sanchirico, Jane Carter Ingram, Glenn-Marie Lange , and Kelly A. Burks-Copes. 2016. The Effectiveness, Costs and Coastal Protection Benefits of Natural and Nature-Based Defences. PLoS ONE. 11 (5). e0154735.

National Committee for Disaster Management (NCDM), Cambodia. n.d. Cambodia_Sendai. Cambodia Disaster Damage & Loss Information System (accessed 17 February 2022).

National Economic and Development Authority (NEDA), Philippines. 2017. *Updated Philippine Development Plan 2017–2022*. Pasig City, Metro Manila.

Nature-based Solutions Initiative (NBSI). 2018. *Evidence Brief: How Effective Are Nature-based Solutions to Climate Change Adaptation?* Prepared by Nathalie Seddon. UK: University of Oxford.

Nauru Maritime and Port Authority (NMPA). n.d. Port Development Project (accessed December 2021).

Nelson, Donald R., Brian P. Bledsoe, Susana Ferreira, and Nathan P. Nibbelink. 2020. Challenges to Realizing the Potential of Nature-Based Solutions. *Current Opinion in Environmental Sustainability*. 45. pp. 49–55.

Oasis. n.d. Oasis Loss Modelling Framework (accessed December 2021).

Office of the Chief Risk Officer, Stanford University, California, USA. Definition of Risk Owner (accessed December 2021).

Oh, Jung Eun, Xavier Espinet Alegre, Raghav Pant, Elco E. Koks, Tom Russell, Roald Schoenmakers , and Jim W. Hall. 2019. *Addressing Climate Change in Transport. Vol 2: Pathway to Resilient Transport*. Vietnam Transport Knowledge Series. Washington, DC: World Bank.

Ohshita, Stephanie, and Kate Johnson. 2017. Resilient Urban Energy: Making City Systems Energy Efficient, Low Carbon, and Resilient in a Changing Climate. Stockholm: European Council for an Energy Efficient Economy.

Overseas Development Institute (ODI). 2013. *Finance for Emergency Preparedness: Links to Resilience*. Working paper written by Katie Peters. London.

Paltan, Homero, Myles Allen, Karsten Haustein, Lena Fuldauer, and Simon Dadson. 2018. Global Implications of 1.5°C and 2°C Warmer Worlds on Extreme River Flows. *Environmental Research Letters*. 13 (9). 094003.

Panwar, V. 2021. Financing Resilient Infrastructure: Bridging the Funding Gap. New Delhi: Coalition for Disaster Resilient Infrastructure.

Roxburgh, Helen. 2017. China's "Sponge Cities" Are Turning Streets Green to Combat Flooding. The Guardian. 28 December.

Rozenberg, Julie, and Marianne Fay. 2019. *Beyond the Gap: How Countries Can Afford the Infrastructure They Need while Protecting the Planet*. Washington, DC: World Bank.

Seddon, Nathalie, Alexandre Chausson, Pam Berry, Cécile A. J. Girardin, Alison Smith, and Beth Turner. 2020. Understanding the Value and Limits of Nature-based Solutions to Climate Change and Other Global Challenges. *Philosophical Transactions of the Royal Society B*. 375 (1794). 20190120.

Silva Zuñiga, Mariana C., Gregory Watson, Graham George Watkins, Amanda Rycerz, and John Firth. 2020. *Increasing Infrastructure Resilience with Nature-Based Solutions (NbS)*. Washington, DC: Inter-American Development Bank.

Sirivunnabood, Pitchaya, and Widya Alwarritzi. 2020. Incorporating a Disaster Risk Financing and Insurance Framework into Country Management and Development Strategies. *Policy Brief*. No. 2020-5. Tokyo: Asian Development Bank Institute.

Smajgl, Alex. 2018. Climate Change Adaptation Planning in Vietnam's Mekong Delta. *Long-term Climate Strategies*. Washington, DC: World Resources Institute.

Sowińska-Świerkosz, Barbara Natalia, and Joan García. 2021. A New Eva,luation Framework for Nature-Based Solutions (NBS) Projects Based on the Application of Performance Questions and Indicators Approach. *Science of the Total Environment*. 787 (2021). 147615.

State Enterprise Policy Office (SEPO), Ministry of Finance, Thailand. 2018. *Public Private Partnership Strategic Plan B.E. 2560-2564 (2017-2021)*. Bangkok.

Sustainable Infrastructure Foundation (SIF). n.d. SOURCE: The Multilateral Platform for Sustainable Infrastructure (accessed December 2021).

Tall, Arame, Sarah Lynagh, Candela Blanco Vecchi, Pepukaye Bardouille, Felipe Montoya Pino, Elham Shabahat, Vladimir Stenek, Fiona Stewart, Samantha Power, Cindy Paladines , Philippe Neves, and Lori Kerr. 2021. *Enabling Private Investment in Climate Adaptation and Resilience*. Washington, DC: World Bank (values for 2017–2018).

Tanner, Thomas, Swenja Surminski, Emily Wilkinson, Robert Reid, Jun Rentschler, and Sumati Rajput. 2015. *The Triple Dividend of Resilience: Realising Development Goals through the Multiple Benefits of Disaster Risk Management*. Global Facility for Disaster Reduction and Recovery (GFDRR) at the World Bank, and Overseas Development Institute (ODI), London.

Tercek, Mark. 2017. Mangroves: A Star Player in the Coastal Protection Game. *Huffington Post*. 9 August.

United Nations Children's Fund (UNICEF) and World Food Programme (WFP). 2015. *UNICEF/WFP Return on Investment for Emergency Preparedness Study: Final Report*. Study done by the Boston Consulting Group, Boston, Massachusetts, USA.

United Nations Climate Change Conference in Glasgow (Scotland) (COP26). 2021. *Climate Change Delivery Plan: Meeting the US$100 Billion Goal*.

United Nations Development Programme (UNDP). 2016. Rapid Integrated Assessment – Cambodia SDG Profile.

———. n.d. Promoting Climate Resilient Infrastructure in Northern Mountain Provinces of Vietnam. (accessed December 2021).

United Nations Development Programme (UNDP) in Cambodia. n.d. Reducing the Vulnerability of Cambodian Rural Livelihoods through Enhanced Sub-National Climate Change Planning and Execution of Priority Actions (SRL) (accessed October 2021).

United Nations Economic and Social Commission for Asia and the Pacific (UN ESCAP) and Asian Institute of Technology (AIT). 2012. *Integrating Environmental Sustainability and Disaster Resilience in Building Codes*. Bangkok and Pathumthani.

United Nations Framework Convention on Climate Change (UNFCCC). n.d.[a]. COP26 Outcomes: Finance for Climate Adaptation (accessed December 2021).

———. n.d.[b]. Introduction to Climate Finance (accessed December 2021).

United Nations Framework Convention on Climate Change (UNFCCC) Standing Committee on Finance. 2021. *Fourth (2020) Biennial Assessment and Overview of Climate Finance Flows*. Bonn.

United Nations Office for Disaster Risk Reduction (UNDRR). 2015. *Sendai Framework for Disaster Risk Reduction 2015–2030*. Geneva.

———. n.d.[a]. Resilience (accessed December 2021).

———. n.d.[b]. Terminology (accessed December 2021).

United Nations Office for Disaster Risk Reduction (UNDRR) Regional Office for Asia and the Pacific and Asian Disaster Preparedness Center (ADPC). 2019. *Disaster Risk Reduction in Cambodia: Status Report 2019*. Bangkok.

University of Washington, Seattle, Washington, USA. n.d. Soil Liquefaction (accessed December 2021).

Vantha, Phoung. 2020. Cambodia Counting the Cost of Recovery from Flooding. *Cambodianess Tmey Thmey in English.* 25 November. Phnom Penh.

Wight, Emily. 2014. Droughts, Flooding, Disease: The Reality of a Cambodia that Has Been Hit by Climate Change. *The Phnom Penh Post.* 11 April.

Willoughby, Christopher. 2002. *Infrastructure and Pro-Poor Growth: Implications of Recent Research.* London: Department for International Development.

Wise, R. M., I. Fazey, M. Stafford Smith, S. E. Park, Hallie Eakin, E. R. M. Archer Van Garderen , and B. Campbell. 2014. Reconceptualising Adaptation to Climate Change as Part of Pathways of Change and Response. *Global Environmental Change.* 28. pp. 325–336.

Woetzel, Jonathan, Dickon Pinner, Hamid Samandari, Hauke Engel, Mekala Krishnan, Brodie Boland , and Carter Powis. 2020. Climate Risk and Response: Physical Hazards and Socioeconomic Impacts. New York: McKinsey Global Institute.

World Bank. 2012. *FONDEN: Mexico's Natural Disaster Fund—A Review.* Washington, DC.

———. 2017. *Climate and Disaster Resilient Transport in Small Island Developing States: A Call for Action.* Washington, DC.

———. 2018. Financing a Resilient Urban Future: A Policy Brief on World Bank and Global Experience on Financing Climate-Resilient Urban Infrastructure. Washington, DC.

———. 2019. $4.2 Trillion Can Be Saved by Investing in More Resilient Infrastructure, New World Bank Report Finds. Press release. 19 June. Washington, DC.

———. 2020a. The Philippines: Transferring the Cost of Severe Natural Disasters to Capital Markets. Feature story. 13 April. Washington, DC.

———. 2020b. Road Connectivity Improvement Project, Cambodia: Procurement Plan.

———. n.d.[a]. Business Enabling Environment (BEE) (accessed December 2021).

———. n.d.[b]. Climate Change Knowledge Portal (accessed December 2021).

World Bank Group (WBG) and Asian Development Bank (ADB). 2021. *Climate Risk Country Profile: Cambodia.* Washington, DC, and Manila.

WorldPop. 2020. Age and Sex Structures (accessed 17 February 2022).

Disaster-resilient Infrastructure
Unlocking Opportunities for Asia and the Pacific

Infrastructure has played a critical role in Asia and the Pacific's rapid economic growth. Roads, bridges, and power networks, among other assets, are part of people's daily lives, and a foundation for their economic opportunity. But increasing disaster risks and climate change is forcing us to rethink how we manage infrastructure. This publication identifies opportunities to deliver resilient infrastructure across developing Asia. It takes a holistic view of practices that affect infrastructure resilience, including risk assessment, investment appraisal, and operation and maintenance across the life cycle of an asset, as well as overarching approaches to achieving system-wide resilience, financing, and governance objectives.

About the Asian Development Bank

ADB is committed to achieving a prosperous, inclusive, resilient, and sustainable Asia and the Pacific, while sustaining its efforts to eradicate extreme poverty. Established in 1966, it is owned by 68 members —49 from the region. Its main instruments for helping its developing member countries are policy dialogue, loans, equity investments, guarantees, grants, and technical assistance.

ISBN 978-92-9269-489-0

ASIAN DEVELOPMENT BANK
6 ADB Avenue, Mandaluyong City
1550 Metro Manila. Philippines
www.adb.org

www.ingramcontent.com/pod-product-compliance
Lightning Source LLC
Chambersburg PA
CBHW042033220326
41599CB00045BA/7295